HC 107 .A13 L94 1989

Lyson, Thomas A.

Two sides to the Sunbelt

TWO SIDES TO THE SUNBELT

TWO SIDES TO THE SUNBELT

The Growing Divergence Between the Rural and Urban South

THOMAS A. LYSON

New York
Westport, Connecticut
London

HC
107
.A13
L94
1989

Library of Congress Cataloging-in-Publication Data

Lyson, Thomas A.
 Two sides to the Sunbelt : the growing divergence between the rural and urban South / Thomas A. Lyson.
  p. cm.
 Bibliography: p.
 Includes index.
 ISBN 0-275-93201-X (alk. paper)
 1. Southern States—Economic conditions—1945- 2. Southern States—Economic policy. 3. Southern States—Rural conditions. I. Title.
 HC107.A13L94 1989
 330.975'043—dc19   88-31928

Copyright © 1989 by Thomas A. Lyson

All rights reserved. No portion of this book may
be reproduced, by any process or technique, without
the express written consent of the publisher.

Library of Congress Catalog Card Number: 88-31928
ISBN: 0-275-93201-X

First published in 1989

Praeger Publishers, One Madison Avenue, New York, NY 10010
A division of Greenwood Press, Inc.

Printed in the United States of America

The paper used in this book complies with the
Permanent Paper Standard issued by the National
Information Standards Organization (Z39.48-1984).

10 9 8 7 6 5 4 3 2 1

*This book is dedicated to my wife
Loretta Carrillo
and my daughters
Mercedes Carrillo Lyson and Helena Carrillo Lyson*

Contents

	Tables and Figures	ix
	Preface	xiii
1.	Economic Development, De Facto Industrial Policies, and the People and Places Left Behind	1
2.	Economic Stagnation in the Rural South: Old Times There Are Not Forgotten	25
3.	Health, Education, and Welfare: Creating and Sustaining Human Capital in the South	49
4.	Industrial Development and Occupational Change: Creating Job Opportunities for Southern Workers	73
5.	Wedding Economic Development to Social Justice	115
	Bibliography	139
	Index	145

Tables and Figures

TABLES

1.1	Selected Development Incentives Available in Eleven Southern States	8
1.2	Selected Characteristics of Labor Market Groups in the South	18
2.1	Poverty Rate of Individuals and Number of Persons in Poverty By Region and Race: 1959, 1975, 1982	27
2.2	Poverty Rates and Changes in the Number of Persons Living in Poverty in North Carolina: 1969–1983	30
2.3	Per Capita Income Comparisons: Black Belt and Rural LMAs as a Percentage of Large Urban LMA and Differences Between the Large Urban LMA and the Black Belt and Rural LMAs	35
2.4	Average Manufacturing Wages by LMA Group: 1967, 1972, and 1982	38
2.5	Average Wages in the Retail Sales and Professional Service Industries in 1980, by LMA Group	40
2.6	Average Unemployment Rates by LMA Group: 1970, 1980, 1982	42
2.7	Average Underemployment Rate by LMA Group: 1970 and 1980	44

3.1	Educational Characteristics of People Over 25 Years Old by LMA Group	53
3.2	Funding and Expenditures for Public Schooling in the South and Distribution of Enrollment by School Type	56
3.3	Infant Mortality Rates and Low Birth Weight Babies by LMA Group	61
3.4	Dentist-to-Population Ratio 1976–1981 by LMA Group	66
3.5	Social Welfare Indicators by LMA Group	68
4.1	Occupational and Industrial Composition of Southern Labor Market Groups (1980)	76
4.2	Percentage Distribution and Average Earnings of Selected Manufacturing Industries by Labor Market Area	80
4.3	Employment Changes in Selected Manufacturing Industries Between 1975 and 1984 by Labor Market Area	82
4.4	Percentage Distribution and Average Earnings of Service Industries by Labor Market Area	86
4.5	Employment Changes in Service Industries Between 1975 and 1984 by Labor Market Area	88
4.6	Distribution of High Technology Employment Across LMA Groups in the South	92
4.7	Occupational Distribution and Average Earnings Per Occupation by Race, Sex, and LMA Group	94
4.8	Occupational Distribution in Manufacturing Industries by Race, Sex, and LMA Group	98
4.9	Occupational Distribution in Service Industries by Race, Sex, and LMA Group	100
4.10	Occupational Distribution in High Technology Industries by Race, Sex, and LMA Group	104
4.11	Distribution of Full-Time and Part-Time Farmers and Income From Farm and Non-Farm Sources by LMA Group	108
4.12	Occupational Characteristics of the Production Agriculture Labor Force by Race, Sex, and LMA Group	110

4.13	Changes in Agribusiness Employment Between 1975 and 1984 and Average Worker Earnings by LMA Group	112
5.1	Decline in Federal Aid Programs to Rural America in Millions of Dollars: 1980–1987	121
5.2	Categories of Public Infrastructure	128

FIGURES

2.1	Poverty Rates by LMA Group: 1969–1979	28
2.2	Per Capita Income by LMA Group: 1969–1983	34
3.1	Characteristics of Teachers in the South	59
3.2	Percentage of Children Born to Teenage Mothers by LMA Group, 1978–1982	62
3.3	Physician-to-Population Ratio by LMA Group (1960–1983)	65

Preface

The impetus for this book came during the mid-1980s while I was living in rural South Carolina and teaching in the Department of Agricultural Economics and Rural Sociology at Clemson University. At that time, I was working on a research monograph with my colleague, Bill Falk, that was designed to document how rural areas of the South had failed to attract their share of the "good" jobs and industries that had spread throughout the Sunbelt during the 1960s and 1970s. Our purpose was to bring the rural South into the industrial policy debate that was taking place then. The findings from our research, reported in *High Tech, Low Tech, No Tech: Recent Occupational and Industrial Changes in the South* (1988, SUNY-Albany Press), showed very clearly that the rural South had been left behind during the region's industrial renaissance.

In fact, although we did not know it at the time, our results presaged the rural crisis that befell the region in the late 1980s. The catalyst behind the socioeconomic demise of the rural South was a set of de facto industrial policies put into place during the 1950s and 1960s. These policies forced rural counties and small towns throughout the South to enter into fierce competition, not only with each other, but with more urban places in the region in the quest for new employers and new jobs. Counties and communities put together various and sundry incentive packages that included tax holidays, subsidized loans, gifts of land and buildings, and vocational training, geared to the specific needs of particular employers. In return, the communities asked for virtually nothing. They requested no guarantees that an employer would hire and keep a certain number of workers on the payroll. They made no stipulation that minorities and women should be hired in proportion to their representation in the labor supply. And they requested no assurances that the employer would remain in the area for a specified time.

Such a one-sided system of giveaways without any assurances that benefits would accrue to the local community clearly invited abuses. Communities were held hostage by firms seeking to eke out even more concessions. The rural South was put into direct competition with Third World countries for footloose industries. And more often than not the rural South could not match the even lower wages, less organized workforce, and unregulated environment that the Third World offered.

As I read the local newspapers and travelled and talked to people in the rural South in the mid-1980s, it became clear to me that not only was the rural South failing to keep pace with the rest of the nation in terms of quality of life and standard of living, it seemed to be falling further behind. Interestingly, however, this growing divergence between the rural and urban South was not readily apparent in the aggregate statistics reported by the federal government and various state agencies. The declining status of rural areas was overshadowed by the achievements of the glittering Sunbelt cities. The booming economies of Atlanta, Charlotte, Jacksonville, Orlando, and scores of other metropolitan areas more than made up for the economic decline in the rural areas. Only when one dug into the aggregate statistics and sorted out the rural from the urban did the two sides of the Sunbelt become clear.

This book is an attempt to document various dimensions to what has become a rural crisis in the South. It is a crisis that rural communities unwittingly helped to create by taking part in the de facto industrial policy game. And unfortunately, it is a crisis that the "new federalism" of the 1980s can do little to remedy. As I outline in the last chapter, it is time for the federal government to step in with both the leadership and resources to alleviate the downward spiral. The rising national economic tide of the 1980s has not lifted all boats. To a greater or lesser extent, predominantly rural and "black belt" areas in the South have failed to ride the crest of the economic development wave that has washed over the region.

Several people were instrumental in helping me prepare this manuscript. Bill Falk, my good friend and colleague at the University of Maryland, helped me to formulate the social justice theme that runs throughout the book. Bill also served as a critical sounding board as I worked through the various analytical chapters. I thank him for his time, suggestions, and insights.

Two longstanding friends and colleagues, Pat Horan at the University of Georgia and Charlie Tolbert at Florida State University, read various drafts of the manuscript and offered their valuable insights into what they saw happening in the rural South. Paul Eberts and Tom Hirschl, my new colleagues at Cornell, listened to my ideas, read various chapters of the book, and made several helpful suggestions. I would like to thank each of them for their time and effort.

Initial funding for this project was provided by the South Carolina Agricultural Experiment Station as part of a Hatch research project (H–1059). After I moved to Cornell University, the Cornell University Agricultural Experiment Station supported this work with Hatch funds in conjunction with USDA/CSRS regional research project S–184.

Organizing and processing the data for a project of this sort is a time consuming and tedious task. Several people affiliated with the Cornell Institute for Social and Economic Research (CISER) made this task considerably easier. Ann Gray, data archivist at CISER, helped me track down the various data sets that I used in my analysis. She kept a watchful eye open for data sources that would not be widely known or available. Much of the richness of the data found in this book is due to Ann's efforts.

Sally Woods, a former research aide at CISER and now a full-time dairy farmer, also helped to find data for this project. Sally also organized the secondary data files into a form that made them easy to analyze.

Lisa King, a research support specialist, and Tom Boggess, computer manager at CISER, know more about doing social science research on an IBM–4381 computer than any two people alive. Without their advice and assistance on the technical aspects of computing at Cornell, this project would still be mired in the nether reaches of the Cornell computer.

Brenda Creely typed and retyped the tables, while Gilles Bergeron ran and reran the graphics. I thank them for their attention to detail, for their ability to meet my sometimes short deadlines, and for their good humor through it all.

Finally, I owe a special debt of gratitude to my family. My wife, Loretta Carrillo, not only put up with my erratic hours, but she read several chapters and commented on various aspects of the project. More importantly, she provided the support and encouragement that I needed to see this project through to the end. When I became too engrossed in detailing the growing divergence between the rural and urban South, our daughters, Mercedes and Helena, helped me to see what is truly important in life. It is to my wife and daughters that I dedicate this book.

TWO SIDES TO THE SUNBELT

1. *Economic Development, De Facto Industrial Policies, and the People and Places Left Behind*

> Economic growth arises from the private sector. But providing the conditions which stimulate and sustain economic growth is properly a significant task of government.[1]

Over the past twenty-five years, industrial recruiters, politicians, and businessmen have sung the praises of the South as a region of bountiful opportunity. They have pointed with pride to the number of new manufacturing and service jobs that have been created in the region. They have touted all of the things that have led the South to the forefront of industrial development. Cheap land, tax abatements of one kind or another, a low wage structure, an unorganized labor force, and a host of other state- and locally sponsored incentives are part and parcel of the "good business climate" that is deemed necessary and sufficient to develop the South.

Along with industrialization came a rising standard of living for many southern families. In 1960, for instance, per capita income in the South was about 60 percent of the national average. By 1970 this gap closed to about 80 percent and by 1980 southern families were earning close to 90 percent of the national average. During the same period, the number of southerners living in poverty also decreased. In 1969, almost 11 million people in the South were poor. These 11 million constituted over 40 percent of all poor people in the United States. By 1979, however, the number of southerners living in poverty had declined by over one million to the point that they only accounted for 36.6 percent of the nation's poor.

The fruits of economic development were not solely confined to income or economic well-being. On virtually all quality-of-life indicators, the differential between the South and the rest of the nation closed. In 1960, for instance, infant mortality among whites exceeded the national average in nine of the 12 southern states and for blacks infant mortality was higher than the national average in 11 of the 12 states. By 1981, infant mortality rates for whites exceeded the national average in only six states, while for blacks only four states had above average infant mortality. On other fronts, life expectancy increased, illiteracy decreased, and the number of homes with indoor plumbing, telephones, and other modern conveniences grew. As economic prosperity washed over the region, many observers predicted that the South could and would soon achieve parity and even surpass the aging industrial regions of the country by the turn of the century.

The South as portrayed in the mass media and hyped by assorted industrial recruiters and frontmen, however, is neither as homogeneous nor as prosperous as it is made out to be. Below the veneer of aggregate statistics and projections and away from the gleeming and growing sunbelt cities, there is another South. It is a South checkered with places that are best characterized by their slow growth, declining industries, and static or falling standard of living. And it is a South populated by persons who have remained relatively untouched by the growth and prosperity that improved the quality of life for many, but not all, of the region's residents. It is found in the "black belt" counties that divide the Piedmont from the Atlantic Coast, that line the Gulf Coast, and that cluster along both banks of the Mississippi River. It exists in the mountain counties of Appalachia. It can be found in the remote nonmetropolitan counties of the Ozarks.

This is the other side of the sunbelt. It is that part that is seldom seen in the glossy advertisements that fill the pages of the nation's business magazines. It consists of places that industrial recruiters often overlook or ignore when they are courting new investment. This other side of the sunbelt is populated by people who have few skills, little education, and little hope of entering the economic mainstream of American society. It is composed of people and places that have been and remain mired in the economic backwaters of the country.

Lionel Beaulieu, a rural sociologist at the University of Florida, recently outlined the social and economic plight of the people and communities in the rural South. Drawing on a broad range of primary and secondary data sources, this is the portrait he paints:

> Low incomes persist in the rural South: Of the 298 nonmetropolitan counties which ranked in the lowest per capita income quintile between 1950 and 1969, 231 remained in this persistent low income classification in 1979; better than 92 percent of these counties were located in the South.
>
> Poverty continues to be highest in rural areas of the South: When contrasted with other regions of the country, poverty levels were higher and median family incomes lower in the South in both 1970 and 1980. In fact, poverty levels in the rural South were still about six percent higher than in any other region of the country in 1980. Present estimates show that 21 percent of the rural southern population are now living in poverty, and the figure is moving upward.
>
> Educational attainment is lowest of any region in the country: The proportion of college graduates in the rural South is 40 percent below the national average. Of the 489 counties in the U.S. having the lowest proportion of adults with a high school education, nearly all are located in the South. Further, functional illiteracy is much higher in the South than the rest of the nation. That is, approximately 25 percent of the adults in the South have less than an eighth grade education, a figure that is substantially higher than the 17 percent uncovered for the remainder of the United States.
>
> Southern rural blacks continue to lag behind: Even with the economic growth of the 1970s, the per capita income of rural black southerners barely reached 30 percent of the U.S. average in 1980. Most telling have been the poverty statistics for these individuals: more than 58 percent of black rural females were living in poverty in 1983; over three-fourths of rural black children under 18 years old living in a female headed household were poor in 1983; and for rural black children under six years of age in a female-headed household, some 80 percent fell below the poverty threshold. Exacerbating the situation has been a southern industrial expansion that essentially has by-passed the bulk of rural areas having sizeable minority populations.[2]

DE FACTO INDUSTRIAL POLICIES: THE ENGINE BEHIND THE GROWTH

To understand how the South was able to make great strides in closing the gap with the rest of the country and yet leave an underclass behind in its wake, one must look first at the sets of policies and programs that were designed and have been put into place over the last 70 years to lure businesses to the region. As early as 1917, for example, Kentucky provided a property tax exemption to manufacturers for machinery and raw materials. Between 1920 and 1930 six other southern states, including Arkansas, Georgia, Louisiana, Mississippi, South Carolina and Virginia, followed suit with their own tax exemption schemes. By way of comparison, in 1930 only three northern states had provisions for any type of tax exemption and in two of these instances the exemption was limited to specific towns or counties.[3]

Mississippi's now legendary Balance Agriculture With Industry (BAWI) program that was instituted in 1936 and later revised in 1944 was the first concerted effort by a state government to "sell" itself to prospective industrialists.[4] Under this program, municipalities were permitted to acquire land and construct buildings for lease to private employers. Funds for these activities were authorized to come from the local municipality itself and from the issuance of general obligation bonds. The BAWI program was an immediate success. Within 10 years of its inception there were 12 BAWI subsidized plants in operation that accounted for 14 percent of Mississippi's industrial work force.

Other southern states followed Mississippi's lead. In 1946 Kentucky authorized municipalities to issue revenue bonds that would be repaid solely by rents. In 1949 the Alabama legislature sanctioned the formation of locally organized industrial development boards to induce new industrial growth. Each board was authorized to issue revenue bonds payable solely from the lessee. By the early 1960s nine southern states were engaged in some form of revenue bond financing.[5]

The use of tax-exempt industrial revenue bonds to attract new industry was the first weapon to be put in the arsenal of financial incentives available to state and local governments. These incentives were soon joined by gifts of land, money, and services. To entice prospective employers to locate in their area, communities would extend sewer and water lines to the industrial site and they would build roads to the site or help finance railroad spur lines.

Tax breaks are another important business incentive and one that can have long-term detrimental consequences for the state and local governments that use them. Whether taxes are lowered across the board as a means of bolstering business confidence in a state, or tax cuts are targetted to new or expanding businesses, the result is often to lower the level of services provided by state and local governments. An exemption from local property taxes, for example, can seriously undercut local school systems, which rely on this revenue source for support. Although no national data are available to assess the amount of revenue forgone by granting tax breaks, it is known that between 1958 and 1961, during the early years of the sunbelt boom, five southern states (Alabama, Kentucky, Louisiana, Mississippi and South Carolina) made tax exemptions worth over $140 million.[6] More recently, South Carolina put together a $16.9 million incentive package to lure a Mack Truck plant to the state. Part of that package was a $2,500 tax credit for each job created.[7] And Kentucky recently offered Toyota a $125 million incentive package that included buying and grading the plant site, building roads, extending utilities, and training workers, in both the United States and Japan.[8]

Revenue bond financing, giveaways of land, money, and services, and tax abatements have not been restricted only to the South, of course. However, during the heyday of industrial growth in the region during the 1960s and 1970s, they were most vigorously exploited by the sunbelt states. The rationale behind the use of subsidies to attract industry is simple enough. They are seen as a necessary cost that states and communities must bear if they are to attract new industry or encourage existing industry to stay and hopefully to expand. Several observers have expressed the belief that business incentives serve a psychological need.[9] They note, for example, that "business incentives are that 'little extra' that may bring industry to a state rather than to its neighbor when they are similar in other respects. In addition, tax incentives and other development policies are the one thing that governments can 'control'."[10]

For the most part, the incentives have been offered to any and all comers to the region without any regard for the long-term consequences of an industrial mix that could in fact impede the ability of the South finally to close the longstanding social and economic gaps with the rest of the nation. Many critics of past economic development efforts have documented, often in amusing detail, the effects these policies have had on the sociopolitical structure of the region.[11]

A prime example of the misguided strategy for industrial development is the textile industry. Still a major source of employment in the region, especially in rural areas, the textile industry is best known for its low wage, unskilled, undereducated, and unorganized workforce. In recent years the industry has fought against the entry of other firms into the region, especially if those businesses are likely to employ workers at wage levels higher than are currently offered in the mills.

In 1984, for instance, Mazda Motor Company announced that it was considering the Greenville/Spartanburg, South Carolina, area as a site for a new auto plant. Eugene Stone, chairman and founder of a textile company that employed over 1500 workers in the local area, wrote to Mazda and asked them not to consider the South Carolina location because such a plant would upset existing wage scales in the area. While it is not known how seriously Mazda took Stone's request, the company ultimately decided to build their plant in Michigan. The Spartanburg Development Association, a local industry-hunting organization, expressed the sentiments of many when it opined in its monthly newsletter: "It is our considered view that the Mazda plant would have had a long-term chilling effect on Spartanburg's orderly industrial growth. An auto plant, employing over 3,000 card-carrying, hymn-singing members of the UAW would, in our opinion, bring to an abrupt halt future desireable industrial prospects."[12]

What has emerged over the years in the South is a set of policies and programs that are best labeled "de facto industrial policies." These policies are built upon a plethora of tangible and intangible business incentives. Orderly planning for industrialization and attention to the "types" of jobs that incentive-seeking businesses create when they move into an area are the cornerstones missing from de facto industrial policies. The primary concern of de facto industrial policymakers is with creating as many jobs as possible. Whether these jobs are white collar or blue collar, high wage or low wage, dead-end or on a promotion track is overshadowed by the overwhelming desire to report job numbers.

In his book, *The Last Entrepreneurs*, Robert Goodman refers to the de facto industrial policy strategy as "legal bribery" and "public entrepreneuring." According to Goodman:

Public entrepreneuring is a different and apparently more legal form of bribery. It is a public payment to business in exchange for business's promise to remain in an area or to relocate to a new one. The bribe makers in this case are government officials, not corporate executives; the offers are not made in dark corners of foreign capitals, through laundered checks or whispered conversations. They are often made in full view, indeed shouted by public officials as loudly as possible so that would-be recipients are able to hear them above the din of other offers.[13]

Perhaps the best source for understanding the nature and range of business incentives offered by state and local governments is the *Site Selection Handbook* put out by Conway Data Inc. Every year, this unabashedly pro-business organization publishes a tally sheet that lists over 60 different business incentives and identifies the states that offer them. Table 1.1 shows how the 12 southern states rate on a sample of ten of these incentives. For comparative purposes and to illustrate how the use of these incentives has spread over the years, 1970 and 1984 data are compared.

A few of the incentives merit a special comment. For example, it is worth noting that every southern state has established a system of vocational training to prepare workers for jobs in new or expanding industries. Since 1961, South Carolina, a pioneer in the area of state-sponsored vocational education, has trained nearly 93,000 people to perform jobs for specific companies. In all, nearly 800 manufacturing plants have benefitted directly from South Carolina's largesse.[14]

In 1984, seven southern states had a publicly sponsored industrial development authority; six states made loans for building construction; four states exempted corporations from state income tax; ten states had programs to promote research and development, while six states provided tax exemptions for research and development activities; and local governments in five states provided free land for incoming plants.

The one incentive that most clearly separates the South from the North is state right-to-work laws. In the South, 11 of 12 states have right-to-work laws. Only Kentucky, with its large cadre of organized mineworkers, is a closed-shop state. Outside of the South, on the other hand, only 9 of 38 states have enacted right-to-work legislation. Right-to-work laws simply mean that a worker in a unionized plant is

Table 1.1
Selected Development Incentives Available in Eleven Southern States

		AL	AR	FL	GA	KY	LA	MS	NC	SC	TN	VA
State Sponsored Industrial Development Authority	1970	X	X			X	X	X	X	X		X
	1984	X	X	X		X	X	X		X		X
City or County Revenue Bond Financing	1970	X	X	X	X	X	X	X	X	X	X	X
	1984	X	X	X	X	X	X	X	X	X	X	X
State Loans for Building Construction	1970					X	X					
	1984			X		X	X	X				
Corporate Income Tax Exemption	1970	X		X	X		X					
	1984	X	X	X	X		X					
State Right to Work Law	1970	X	X	X	X			X	X	X	X	X
	1984	X	X	X	X		X	X	X	X	X	X

City or Counties Provide Free Land for Industry	1970							X	X	
	1984	X					X	X	X	X
State Recruiting and Screening of Industrial Employees	1970		X	X	X		X	X	X	X
	1984		X	X	X		X	X	X	X
State Program to Promote Research and Development	1970		X	X	X		X	X	X	
	1984		X	X			X	X	X	X
Tax Exemption for Research and Development Activities	1970									
	1984	X		X		X	X	X		X

Sources: *Site Selection Handbook, Geo-Political Index.* September 1984, Vol. 29, No. 3. Conway Data Incorporated.

1970 Site Selection Handbook, Vol. 2. Conway Research, Inc., Atlanta, Georgia.

under no obligation to join that union, even though he or she may benefit from the union's activities. For firms that are trying to run away from unions, right-to-work states make excellent hiding places. All of the right-to-work states noted in Table 1.1 have unionization rates far below the national average.[15]

North Carolina and South Carolina regularly vie with one another to see which state can report the smallest percentage of unionized workers and the least number of days lost to strikes. Today, less than seven percent of the nonagricultural workforce in the two states belongs to unions, and most of the union workers are employees of the federal government. The rabid anti-union sentiment in the Deep South was recently noted by James Cobb when he wrote:

> By the end of the 1970s antiunionism had supplanted racism as the South's most respectable prejudice. Senator Strom Thurmond of South Carolina, a former segregationist, found it easier to cope with black voting than with the threat of unionization. Said one labor leader, "He'll accept blacks now, but you still don't see Strom shaking hands with union people."[16]

The states that have enacted the types of programs and policies listed in Table 1.1 have registered impressive short-term gains in creating new job opportunities and improving the quality of life of their workers. Certainly aggregate statistics for wages, income, and job creation for the South have shown marked improvement over the past two decades. Yet despite these impressive gains, the boom that has swept over the sunbelt is not all that it could have or should have been.

This book focuses on those people and places that have experienced little or no benefit or prosperity from the influx of industries and jobs that have come into the region over the past two decades. These are the people and places that are lost or overlooked in the aggregate statistics that are popularly used to reference the progress the South has made in entering the mainstream of the American economy. It is my contention that the *type* of economic development policies southern leaders pursued in their efforts to bring jobs to the region are part and parcel of the problem. The de facto industrial policies that have pitted state against state and community against community in the quest for new jobs have benefitted some, but not all, southerners.

To a greater or lesser extent, women, blacks, and persons from rural areas have remained disproportionately concentrated in the underclass.

I am concerned with understanding the underlying reasons why some people and places rode the crest of economic development while others were left behind. It is not my purpose, however, to point a finger or pin blame on those persons who formulated and put into place the various and sundry de facto policies. Rather, my aim is to place the policies that have guided economic development in the region within a larger theoretical framework, a framework that can simultaneously account for the rising standard of living for southern workers and communities evident in the aggregate statistics, and the existence of a group of people and places that remain untouched by the benefits brought forth by the de facto industrial policies.

ECONOMIC GROWTH AND SOCIAL JUSTICE

In simple terms, this is a book about economic growth and social justice. While these two concepts are not incompatible with one another, it does not necessarily follow that programs and policies that stimulate economic growth ensure that social and economic justice is served. In fact, in many cases just the opposite may occur. As we look in the coming chapters at the progress southern leaders have made over the past quarter of a century in attracting industries and jobs to the region, one would have to conclude that they have been very successful in stimulating economic growth. At the same time, however, as the average standard of living and quality of life of workers in the region have improved, the benefits of this economic growth have, in many cases, not "trickled down" to those at the bottom of the economic ladder. For these people, the de facto industrial policies have produced neither economic opportunity nor social justice.

An assumed tradeoff between economic growth and social justice has pervaded development efforts in the sunbelt and has served to rationalize the inability of de facto industrial policies to bring the most disadvantaged groups into the economic mainstream. De facto industrial policies implicitly rest upon the notion that economic development is a contest that pits one locality against another. The "prize" in this contest is a new industry or firm and the jobs it brings with it.

To enter into this game, communities must arm themselves with an arsenal of business incentives. Much like a high stakes poker game, one community's incentives are bid against another community's incentives in an effort to "win" a new employer. In this game, however, there may be no real winners. Obviously, states and towns that invest in incentives of one sort or another and fail to stimulate new economic growth are losers. But localities that get carried away in their efforts to lure new businesses and sweeten the pot too much may find that they have bartered away their ability to improve the lot of the most disadvantaged people. Rural communities, small towns, and less affluent counties, because they have fewer "chips" to offer prospective employers, are certainly placed in a structurally disadvantaged position in this game. In short, these places have become trapped at the bottom of a system that they unwittingly helped to create.

The extent to which states will compete against one another to attract wayward manufacturing firms is well documented. The following vignette is typical of the infighting that can occur. In the early 1970s an upstate New York community was in line to acquire an aluminum manufacturing plant that was looking to leave Pennsylvania. The New York Industrial Agency, along with the State Commerce Department and local development officials, helped the firm find a suitable plant site and were in the process of arranging industrial revenue bond financing when the owner of the plant received a call from the governor of South Carolina. According to the owner, "He [the Governor] said that he heard that I was trying to locate a plant and he wondered if he could fly up in his personal jet, pick me up, and fly me down to South Carolina to show me what they had to offer."[17]

What South Carolina had to offer was a building that was 30 years newer than the one in New York at one-fifth the cost. South Carolina also offered a 10-year moratorium on most taxes. This reduced the tax bill to $2,000/year compared with a projected tax bill of $79,000/year in New York. To top it all off, South Carolina also offered to pay the cost of moving the company to the state, and the costs of training all of the workers hired. Not surprisingly, the company moved to South Carolina.[18]

This example clearly shows that decisions about plant location are *not* the product of free market forces. The government-subsidized incentives offered by state and local officials can and do play a key role. Furthermore, the incentives have a real cost to the residents of the states and localities offering them in terms of forgone public services such as special education programs and amenities such as water and sewer systems.

To illustrate how quickly this bidding for business can get out of hand, one need only look at the efforts of the Arkansas Industrial Development Commission (AIDC) during the late 1950s and early 1960s. During this time, AIDC staff members culled through the financial records of 300,000 firms listed in the Dunn and Bradstreet Financial Reports on American Industry and identified 30,000 who had a bond rating of B or higher. Each of these 30,000 was then contacted to see if they might possibly consider Arkansas for future expansion. From the 30,000 an "active" prospect file was developed. Each of these firms was then contacted personally by AIDC staff. The AIDC estimated that between 1955 and 1962 their plant location consultants had called or called back more than 60,000 times on industries seeking to keep up-to-date with those interested in new plant locations. As the AIDC proudly proclaimed in their 1963 Annual Report, "It can be safely said without fear of contradiction that no other state in the nation has developed or even approached such an intense program of personal solicitation for new industry."[19] One might wonder how many new Arkansas plants resulted from the 60,000 phone calls. The answer is 523.[20] Of course, there is no way of knowing how many of the 523 would have located in Arkansas without the intense solicitation. However, it is known that other southern states such as North Carolina and South Carolina fared at least as well as Arkansas in the quest for new jobs, even though neither had mounted such an extensive campaign of personal contact.

Despite the almost Herculean efforts by southern industrial recruiters to attract jobs, the benefits that accrued to the states were very unevenly distributed. Some places gained jobs, while other areas stagnated or declined. Some groups of workers were able to partake of the new opportunities while others were barred from them. From my perspective, economic justice is served only when the industrial development programs and policies work to the direct benefit of everyone, particularly the least advantaged. To paraphrase John Rawls, a leading authority on the subject of justice, if one wishes to judge whether economic development policies are just, these policies must be examined from the point of view of those at the bottom of the economic ladder. Only when economic development policies enhance the opportunities and life chances of those at the bottom can they be considered just.[21]

Phrased a bit differently, Rawls' notion of justice is grounded on the belief that all social goods including income, wealth, and opportunity should be distributed on an equitable basis. Social and economic inequalities are permitted in a society only if they are arranged to the greatest benefit of the least advantaged members of that society.[22] Discussing this principle of justice, Tom Beauchamp notes, "... this principle expresses Rawls's conviction that the justice of the basic structure is to be gauged by its tendency to counteract the inequalities caused purely by luck of birth (family and class origin), natural endowment and historical circumstance (accidents over the course of a lifetime)."[23] Rawls' theory, then, is clearly egalitarian since it requires society to reduce certain inequalities by pooling resources for everyone's benefit, especially those who are least advantaged.

Concern with the relationship between economic development and social justice has recently been brought to the forefront of American domestic policy by the Catholic Church. The U.S. Bishops' "Pastoral Letter on Catholic Social Teaching and the U.S. Economy" was written to provide guidance for members of the Catholic Church as they seek to reach moral decisions about economic matters and to add the Church's voice to the public debate about U.S. economic policies. In judging economic policies, the Bishops' letter is guided by one fundamental norm: "What will this approach or policy do to the poor and deprived members of the human community?"[24]

While some sections of the Bishops' document rest on biblical and theological foundations, many of the arguments for economic justice are developed in a reasoned secular manner that is designed to persuade persons who do not share the Catholic faith or the Christian tradition. The Bishops note, for example, that in the United States the long-term poor are disproportionately concentrated among blacks, female-headed families, and persons from rural areas, small towns, and/or the South. These are the groups that have benefitted the least from the de facto industrial policies. Drawing on theories of economic justice, the Pastoral Letter articulates three priority principles that must be invoked to assist these people. First, the fulfillment of the basic needs of the poor is of the highest priority. Second, increased participation of these "marginalized" groups takes priority over the preservation of privileged concentrations of wealth, power, and income. And third, meeting the needs of those at the bottom of the economic hierarchy should be a priority target in the investment of wealth, talent, and human energy.[25]

Virtually all existing de facto industrial policies would be hard-pressed to pass the test of economic justice put forth by Rawls and the Catholic Bishops. This is not to say that de facto industrial policies cannot be defended from a moral position. For instance, current de facto policies are typically justified on utilitarian principles of social justice.

Without going into a great amount of detail, let me briefly articulate the economic justice components of two popular versions of utilitarianism—classic utilitarianism and average utilitarianism—as they apply to the distribution of opportunities and rewards associated with economic development. According to classic utilitarianism, industrial policies of whatever variety can be considered as just if they operate to enhance the *overall* life chances of the population in question. From a practical standpoint, this means that de facto industrial policies are considered just if they succeed merely in attracting new businesses and jobs to an area or encouraging existing firms to expand employment. Under average utilitarianism, justice is measured by dividing the benefits of industrial development policy by the number of persons affected by those policies. In reality, average utilitarianism and classic utilitarianism are identical when the population is stable. In both cases, attention is directed toward the creation of job opportunities and not the allocation of these opportunities among the population. In other words, there is no assurance that those segments of the population most in need of assistance or jobs will receive these benefits.

Consequently, in neither the classic nor the average case does utilitarianism expressly deal with or address the plight of the underclass. Their lot in life may or may not appreciably improve under a de facto industrial policy agenda. Utilitarianism, then, can be considered nonegalitarian to the extent that it justifies *any* distribution of social goods as long as it maximizes average or total utility, however unequal that distribution may be. Holly Smith Goldman illustrates this facet of utilitarianism when she asks us to "... imagine a society which must choose between two arrangements, in the first of which the worst-off persons receive an annual income of five hundred dollars while the best-off persons receive five million, and in the second of which the worst-off persons receive five thousand while the best-off persons receive fifty thousand. If the first of these arrangements would maximize average utility, then utilitarianism prescribes it even though it involves far greater disparity between economic classes than the second."[26]

As the above discussion illustrates, it is not too difficult to see that job creation guided only by de facto industrial policies may not enhance the standard of living of *all* southern workers. The *types* of jobs that are created when industry moves south and the distribution of these new jobs across rural and urban areas and among various segments of the population are issues that are largely ignored by the utilitarian/de facto perspective.

In this book, I will demonstrate that to a greater or lesser extent, rural and small town residents along with women and blacks have failed to ride the crest of economic development that has washed over the region. These are the segments of the population that the Catholic Bishops and various policymakers have identified as being most in need of attention.

LABOR MARKET AREAS IN THE SOUTH

To understand what has happened to the people and places left behind during the 1970s and 1980s, and to provide a basis for policy intervention, it is useful to partition the South into groups of counties that share similar social and economic characteristics. In selecting relevant criteria to classify counties I was guided by previous work in this area, especially the scheme used by Falk and Lyson in their study of occupational and industrial change in the South since 1970,[27] the one used by Horan and Tolbert in their study of rural labor markets in the region,[28] and the classification developed by the Southern Growth Policies Board to study changing employment patterns in the region.[29]

The fundamental unit of analysis in the present inquiry is the "labor market area" or "LMA." The LMA concept was developed by Charles Tolbert[30] and others under the auspices of the Economic Research Service of the United States Department of Agriculture. Without going into a great amount of technical detail, it should be noted that LMAs are county groups formulated on the basis of journey-to-work data from the 1980 U.S. Census of Population. A hierarchical cluster analysis of county-to-county flows of commuters was used to group counties into areas of at least 100,000 inhabitants.[31]

Labor market areas, as defined by Tolbert and used here, are substantively different from the other county group schema discussed above. By forming county groups on the basis of commuter flows, the geographic area that is delimited represents an area that encompasses both the place of residence and the place of work of a local population. Furthermore, if we accept the common definition of a LMA as being composed of "buyers" (employers) and "sellers" (employees) of labor, then the LMA can be considered a geographic proxy that represents a set of exchange relations.

Tolbert and his colleagues identified 382 distinct LMAs in the United States. Of these 382, there are 128 LMAs in the 11 southern states that are the focus of this inquiry. For the sake of parsimony, and to facilitate examining issues of social justice and economic development, I have chosen to group these 128 LMAs into five groups based on three salient demographic characteristics: 1) population size; 2) the percentage of the population in the LMA that is black; and 3) the percentage of the LMA that resides in urban places. Table 1.2 lists the five LMA groups that are formed using these criteria.

Three of the groups of LMAs have a substantial urban component (over 40 percent of the population lives in an urban place) and have populations that are predominantly white (over 60 percent of the population is white). One group of these urban LMAs consists of the largest LMAs in the region—those with over 1,000,000 residents. These LMAs, labeled "large urban" LMAs in Table 1.2, are anchored on a large central city such as Atlanta, Miami, or New Orleans and include the surrounding counties.

A second group of urban LMAs consists of LMAs with between 500,000 and one million residents. These are labeled "mid-size urban" LMAs in Table 1.2. Included here are areas dominated by cities such as Charlotte (North Carolina), Jacksonville (Florida), and Nashville (Tennessee).

The third group of urban/white labor markets are labeled "small urban" LMAs in Table 1.2. They consist of areas with between 100,000 and 500,000 inhabitants. Typical LMAs in this category include areas surrounding Asheville (North Carolina), Augusta (Georgia), and Sarasota (Florida).

In addition to these three highly urban and predominantly white labor market groups, two other labor market clusters are also identified. One group is composed of LMAs that are highly rural (over 60 percent of the inhabitants live in rural places) and predominantly

Table 1.2
Selected Characteristics of Labor Market Groups in the South

	Urban LMA's			Rural	Black Belt
	Large	Mid-Size	Small		
Number of LMA's	8	16	59	36	9
1984 Population	12,935,277	11,100,924	17,366,057	7,780,950	1,978,582
1980 Population	11,999,024	11,607,518	17,058,677	7,564,651	1,950,631
1970 Population	9,471,940	9,703,660	14,477,763	6,187,747	8,811,358

Δ % 1980-1984	7.8	6.1	5.3	4.6	2.1
Δ % 1970-1980	26.7	19.6	17.8	22.2	7.7
% Black (1980)	20.6	22.3	21.0	11.8	46.9
% Below Poverty (1980)	13.7	13.9	16.8	18.6	26.3
% Urban (1980)	86.3	66.8	57.5	29.5	44.5

Source: County and City Data Book, various years.

white. This group is called simply "rural" in Table 1.2. LMAs in this group are scattered throughout the sunbelt, but are mostly concentrated in the Upland South and in the Appalachian section of the region.

The final group of LMAs is labeled the "black belt." These LMAs have high concentrations of black residents (over 40 percent black). They are located primarily in the old plantation area of the South and form a loose band that extends from Virginia across the low country of North Carolina, South Carolina, and into Georgia, Alabama, and Mississippi.

AN OVERVIEW OF CONDITIONS IN THE LABOR MARKET GROUPS

It should be clear to most readers that the classification of labor market types is designed to approximate a continuum of socioeconomic conditions and opportunity in the South. The large and mid-size urban LMAs are the most favored in terms of jobs, income, and standard of living, while the rural and black belt LMAs are the least favored. This presentation of labor market groups should be useful to policymakers, program planners, and others interested and concerned about economic development in the region. Table 1.2 presents some aggregate social, economic, and demographic measures to illustrate some basic differences among the LMA groups.

The "large urban" category consists of eight separate LMAs. The largest of these is the Miami LMA, with over 2.7 million inhabitants. The smallest is Birmingham, Alabama, with just over one million residents. Taken together, this group manifested the most rapid growth during the 1970s. The combined population expanded by over 2.5 million persons. Not surprisingly, this is the most highly urbanized of the five groups. Over 85 percent of the inhabitants live in an urban area. Overall, about two in ten residents in the large LMAs are black. Finally, the poverty rate in this LMA category is the lowest among the five LMA groups.

The "mid-size urban" group is similar in many respects to the large LMA group. Both have relatively low poverty rates. The percentage of the population that is black is about the same. And both groups have about the same number of inhabitants. The mid-size urban LMAs, however, grew a bit slower during the 1970s than the large

LMAs. Also, the mid-size urban LMAs have somewhat fewer urban residents than the large LMA group.

The "small urban" LMA group is composed of 59 different LMAs in the South. This is clearly the modal category and not surprisingly, has the largest number of inhabitants—over 17 million. Despite the large population size, this group grew slower than any of the other LMA groups except the black belt. This group of LMAs is also a bit more rural than the other urban labor market groups and the poverty rate is higher. Like the other two urban LMA categories, however, about 20 percent of the population is black.

The "rural" LMA group consists of 36 LMAs. These range in population from just over 100,000 to over 400,000. The distinguishing characteristic is that in all instances over 60 percent of the population resides in rural areas. Taken together, seven in ten residents in this group live outside of a city or town. These areas grew by over 22 percent between 1970 and 1980. In spite of this impressive growth, however, nearly 20 percent of the rural LMA population lives at or below the poverty line. Only the black belt has a higher poverty rate.

The final LMA group in Table 1.2 is the "black belt." There are nine LMAs in this group. Together, they are composed of 71 counties. Most are small LMAs with between 100,000 and 200,000 residents. This group of LMAs manifested the slowest growth between 1970 and 1980. Over half of the inhabitants live in rural areas. And the poverty rate is nearly double that found in the large and mid-size urban LMAs.

A NOTE ON DATA PRESENTATION

In general, data will be presented as the average of the LMA means for each of the five LMA subgroups. That is, statistical means will be computed for each LMA within each LMA group (i.e., large urban, mid-size urban, etc.). The means are then averaged within each of the five groups. Thus, the N for reporting data will typically be 9 for the black belt LMA group, 36 for the rural LMA group, and so forth. Reporting data in this fashion provides a picture of the "typical" LMA within each of the five analytical groups. Further, this procedure has the effect of standardizing for size of the LMA, since each LMA in a group is weighted equally in the tabulations.

Occasionally, however, it will be necessary to report data not as LMA averages, but as averages of individuals within the five LMA groups. Here the various LMAs that are used to define the five LMA groups are not used in computing percentages. Rather, individuals within all LMAs in the group are the reporting units. This procedure is used when there are missing data for various LMAs. Based on the assumption that there is more social and economic homogeneity within LMA groups than between LMA groups, the use of individuals rather than LMAs in computing final percentages should not confound the results.

PLAN OF THE BOOK

In the next three chapters I will examine various facets of social and economic change in the five labor market groups. While the data to be presented in the following chapters will be organized primarily around groups of LMAs, when appropriate, I will examine variations within each of the five analytical groups as well. I will draw on a wide range of data including material from the U.S. Census of Population, the U.S. Census of Agriculture, County and City Data Book, County Business Patterns, and various machine-readable data files (e.g., County Statistics, Volume 2 [COSTAT II], Area Resource File [ARF]) and the like. My timeframe will center primarily on the period after 1970, although at times I will use data dating back to the 1950s and 1960s to bolster my arguments. My intent is to establish the nature of inequalities among and within the various labor market groups and to assess changes in these inequalities over time. Toward this end, I will probe changes in aggregate measures of economic well-being and opportunity across the labor market groups as well as examine how various race and sex subpopulations fare within each of the county groups.

Chapter 2 focuses on indices of social and economic well-being. Special attention will be paid to per capita income, wage rates, poverty, and unemployment and underemployment. Chapter 3 looks at human capital and social welfare characteristics within and among the county groups. Here I will examine various measures of educational attainment, schooling expenditures, school facilities, single-parent and female-headed families, healthcare measures such as infant mortality, teenage pregnancy, and the like. Chapter 4 deals with employment opportunities. The focus here will be on examining the nature and range of jobs that have been created in the different county groups in recent years and the distribution of those jobs across race and sex groups. Special attention will also be paid to the agricultural and farm workforce in the region.

I conclude the book with a chapter titled "Wedding Economic Development and Social Justice." In this chapter I summarize the findings from the previous three analytical chapters and suggest ways to move from a system of self-defeating and shortsighted de facto industrial policies to a more unified, coherent, and "just" program of economic development.

NOTES

1. Moody's Investors Service, Inc., 1968, *Opportunity and Growth in South Carolina 1968-1985*, New York: Moody's Investor Service.

2. Beaulieu, Lionel J., 1988, "The Rural South in Crisis: An Introduction," in L. J. Beaulieu (ed.), *The Rural South in Crisis* (Boulder, CO: Westview), pp. 1-12.

3. Martin, James W., 1931, "Industrial Change and Taxation Problems in the Southern States," *Annals of the American Academy of Political and Social Science* 153 (January): 224-237.

4. Cobb, James C., 1982, *The Selling of the South* (Baton Rouge: Louisiana State University Press).

5. Cobb, James C., 1984, *Industrialization and Southern Society 1877-1984* (Lexington, KY: University Press of Kentucky).

6. Ibid.

7. Myers, Greg, 1986, "States Wage Costly Wars for New Industries," *Greenville News/Piedmont* (March 4).

8. Ingwerson, Marshall, 1986, "Japanese Firms Help South Rise Again," *Christian Science Monitor* (May 6).

9. See, for example, Neil Pierce, 1979, "State 'Smokestack Chasing'—Barking Up the Wrong Tree?" *Washington Post* (June 3).

10. Walsh, Susan M., and Craig M. Wheeland, 1984, "Tax Incentives for Industrial and Economic Development," in C. B. Graham, Jr. and C. B. Tyer (eds.), *Local Government in South Carolina: Problems and Perspectives* (Columbia, SC: University of South Carolina, Bureau of Governmental Research and Service), pp. 153-70.

11. See for example, Cobb, 1982, *The Selling of the South*; Cobb, 1984, *Industrialization*; and Thomas H. Naylor and James Clotfelter, 1975, *Strategies for Change in the South* (Chapel Hill: University of North Carolina Press).

12. "Saved from Mazda," 1985, *Greenville News* (January 11).

13. Goodman, Robert, 1979, *The Last Entrepreneurs* (New York: Simon and Schuster).

14. Vass, Kathy, 1986, "TEC Tailors Classes to Industries' Needs," *Greenville News/Piedmont* (May 11).

15. Hirschl, Thomas A., Gene F. Summers, and Leonard E. Bloomquist, 1989, "Right to Work Legislation and Local Labor Market Growth," in W. W. Falk and T. A. Lyson (eds.) *Research in Rural Sociology and Development.* Volume 4: *Focus on Rural Labor Markets* (Greenwich, CT: JAI Press).

16. Cobb, 1982, *The Selling of the South*, p. 259.

17. McKeating, Michael P., 1975, "New York Losing the Race for New Industry," *Empire State Report* 1 (October): 378. Reprinted in Peter D. McClelland and Alan L. Magdovitz, 1981, *Crisis in the Making* (Cambridge, MA: Cambridge University Press).

18. Ibid.

19. *Report*, 1963, Arkansas Industrial Development Commission (Little Rock, Arkansas).

20. Ibid.

21. Rawls, John, 1971, *A Theory of Justice* (Cambridge: Harvard University Press).

22. Ibid., p. 302.

23. Beauchamp, Tom L., 1980, "Distributive Justice and the Difference Principle," in H. G. Blocker and E. H. Smith (eds.), *John Rawls' Theory of Social Justice* (Athens, OH: Ohio University Press), pp. 132-61.

24. U.S. Bishops' Pastoral Letter on Catholic Social Teaching and the U.S. Economy. First Draft published in *Origins* 14 (22/23), November 15, 1984.

25. Ibid.

26. Goldman, Holly Smith, 1980, "Rawls and Utilitarianism," in Blocker and Smith (eds.), *John Rawls' Theory*, pp. 346-94.

27. Falk, W. W., and T. A. Lyson, 1987, *Hi-Tech, Low-Tech, No-Tech: Recent Economic Changes in the Rural and Urban South* (Albany: SUNY-Albany Press).

28. Horan, Patrick M., and Charles M. Tolbert, 1984, *The Organization of Work in Rural and Urban Labor Markets* (Boulder, CO: Westview Press).

29. Rosenfeld, Stuart A., Edward M. Bergmar, and Sarah Rubin, 1985, *After the Factories* (Research Triangle Park, NC: Southern Growth Policies Board).

30. See especially Charles M. Tolbert and Molly Sizer Killean, 1987, "Labor Market Areas in the United States," Economic Research Service, United States Department of Agriculture (Washington, D.C.) and Charles M. Tolbert, 1987, "Labor Market Areas in Stratification Research: Concepts, Definitions, and Issues," in W. W. Falk and T. A. Lyson (eds.) *Research in Rural Sociology and Development*, Volume 4.

31. Ibid.

2. Economic Stagnation in the Rural South: Old Times There Are Not Forgotten

> On the surface the rural South seems to promise much in terms of quality of life. It is uncrowded; the climate is mild; natural beauty abounds; the air is clean; and the water relatively unpolluted. Closer examination reveals that this is an area of economic stagnation and decline. . . . For many who live there, the rural South is a slum as dreadful in its own way as a big city ghetto.[1]

In 1967 President Lyndon Johnson's National Advisory Commission on Rural Poverty issued a report that brought into sharp focus the chronic economic status of rural areas in the United States. That report, "The People Left Behind," concluded that ". . . rural poverty is so widespread and so acute, as to be a national disgrace."[2] The report also noted that ". . . most of the rural South is one vast poverty area."[3] Twenty years later most of the rural South is still mired in the backwaters of the American economy with per capita incomes well below the national average and poverty rates that are two to three times those found elsewhere in the country.

Although economic conditions in the rural South remain bleak, impressive gains were made in alleviating poverty in both the urban and rural areas of the region during the 1960s and early 1970s. Overall, the poverty rate in the South fell from 35.4 percent of the population in 1959 to 16.2 percent in 1975. For blacks, the decline was even more dramatic. In 1959, 68.5 percent of all southern blacks lived in poverty. By 1975, the percentage of blacks living below the poverty line had fallen to 36.5 percent. The proportion of white southerners living in poverty also fell from 26.8 percent in 1959 to 11.4 percent in 1975.

It is generally agreed that the decline in the poverty rate in the South resulted not so much from the growth of new, high-wage employment opportunities in the region, but rather from a massive out-migration of poor blacks (and to a lesser extent poor whites) to the industrial cities of the Northeast and Midwest. The impetus behind this out-migration was the shifting of cotton production, the bedrock of the rural economy in the Deep South, out of the region. The number of cotton farms in Mississippi, a state long synonymous with cotton production, for instance, declined 96.8 percent, from 156,249 in 1954 to just 4992 in 1978. Other equally dramatic declines in the number of cotton farms took place during this time in every other southern state. As cotton production drifted out of the region, it left in its wake a sea of displaced and poverty-stricken sharecroppers and tenant farmers. With their source of livelihood taken from them, and with little hope that the local economy could generate a sufficient number of other employment alternatives to keep them in the area, vast numbers left the South in search of employment in the North.

The data in Table 2.1 neatly illustrate how the South was able to show improvement in reducing poverty without really improving economic opportunities. In 1960 the black population in the United States stood at 18.8 million persons and over 60 percent of them lived in the South. Furthermore, there were almost 10 million blacks living in poverty in the United States in 1960 and over three-fourths of them lived in the South. Today the black population has grown to over 26 million persons and the percentage living in the South has declined to 53 percent. And despite the fact that there are still 10 million blacks living in poverty, the number of southern blacks in poverty has fallen to 5.8 million (a decline of 1.8 million since 1960).

Looked at a bit differently, in 1959 three-fourths of all blacks living in poverty resided in the South. By 1982 only 56.6 percent of all poor blacks were southerners. In terms of absolute numbers, the number of poor southern blacks declined from 7.5 million to 5.5 million between 1959 and 1982 while the number of non-southern blacks living in poverty increased from 2.5 million in 1959 to 4.3 million in 1982.

Table 2.1
Poverty Rate of Individuals and Number of Persons in Poverty By Region and Race: 1959, 1975, 1982

		Non-South		South		% of Poor Residing in the South	
		White	Black	White	Black	White	Black
1959	Poverty Rate (%)	14.8	34.3	26.8	68.5	40.5	75.6
	N in Poverty (mil)	17.0	2.5	11.5	7.5		
1975	Poverty Rate (%)	9.0	25.2	11.4	36.5	35.1	62.4
	N in Poverty (mil)	11.5	2.8	6.2	4.7		
1982	Poverty Rate (%)	11.3	33.3	13.4	37.6	35.3	56.6
	N in Poverty (mil)	14.0	4.3	9.5	5.5		

Source: U.S. Bureau of the Census "Characteristics of the Population Below the Poverty Level: 1982." Current Population Reports (Series P-60, No. 144). Washington, DC: U.S. Government Printing Office, 1984. Table 4.

The percentage of poor whites who live in the South, on the other hand, shows a more modest decline between 1959 and 1982. In 1959, 40.5 percent of all whites living in poverty resided in the South. By 1975, this figure had fallen only to about 35 percent. And since 1975, the proportion of poor whites residing in the South appears to have stabilized.

By the mid 1970s much of the exodus of poor people out of the region had subsided. While the rural South was able to "export" many of its poor to the North, it was by no means able to discard all of them. The data in Figure 2.1 show that in 1969 the average poverty rate among the black belt LMAs was 38.6 percent. This was over twice the rate found in the large and mid-size urban LMAs. Only the rural LMAs, with an average poverty rate of 26.9 percent, came close to the black belt.

Figure 2.1
Poverty Rates by LMA Group 1969-1979

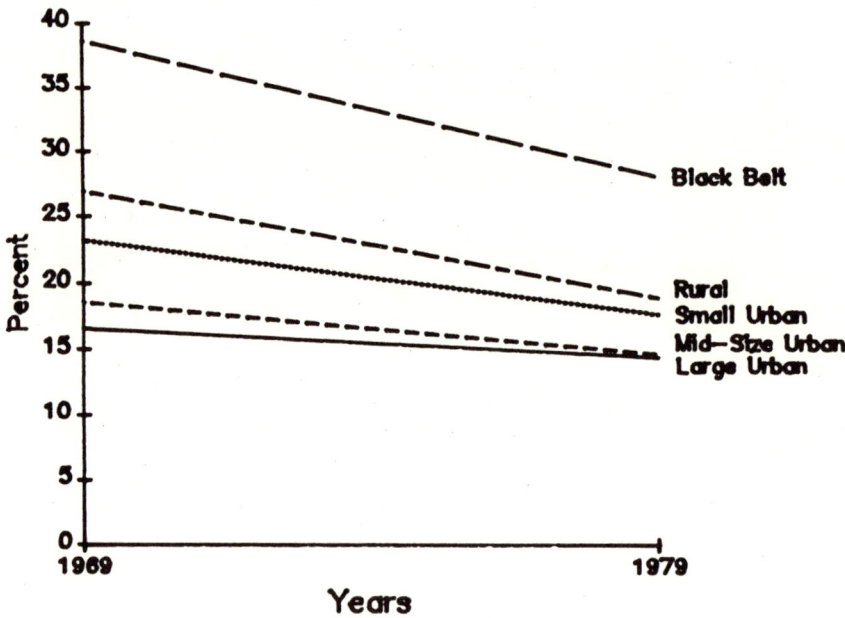

Source: U.S. Census of Population, 1970 and 1980.

Between 1969 and 1979 all of the labor market groups showed declines in poverty. Yet the disparities evident in 1969 among the five LMA groups were maintained throughout the decade. The black belt still had a poverty rate nearly twice that found in the large and mid-size urban LMAs. And as the data in Figure 2.1 indicate, the average poverty rate among the black belt LMAs in 1979 was *higher* than the poverty rate was in any other LMA group in 1969.

An interesting caveat must be noted here. The declining poverty rate among the LMAs between 1969 and 1979 did not necessarily mean that the number of poor people declined in all of the LMAs. For instance, despite a decline in the poverty rate in the large urban LMAs from 16.6 percent in 1969 to 14.4 percent in 1979, the number of poor people in these labor market areas actually increased from 1.52 million to 1.64 million persons. Much of this increase was concentrated in the inner-city areas of these large urban LMAs. In fact, the poverty rate in four of the eight center-city counties associated with the large urban LMAs (Louisville, Atlanta, Miami, and New Orleans) actually increased between 1969 and 1979. At least part of the increase in the number of inner city poor people is due to the influx of migrants from the black belt. The black population of Atlanta, for instance, increased by over 150,000 during the 1970s. Between 1980 and 1985 another 57,000 were added to the population. At the same time, the black belt was losing people. From 1983 to 1985, 26 of Georgia's 50 black belt counties lost population.[4]

Overall, the poverty rate in the large urban LMAs went down not because the number of poor people decreased, but because the number of non-poor increased faster than the number of poor increased. In the other four LMA groups, the number of poor decreased, but not to the extent that the change in poverty rates from 1969 to 1979 might suggest.

The intractability of the poverty problem in the South is further illustrated by the fact that in 1969 all nine of the black belt LMAs had poverty rates over 25 percent, whereas none of the eight large urban LMAs had this degree of poverty. Ten years later, in 1979, seven of the nine of the black belt LMAs still had poverty rates in excess of 25 percent. No large or mid-size urban LMA had this degree of poverty and less than ten percent of the LMAs in the small urban and rural groups had rates this high.

Since 1979, poverty rates have begun to rise again in both the rural and urban South due in part to the lingering effects of the 1981/82 recession and to the farm crisis that devastated rural areas of the region between 1982 and 1986. In many places there are more people living in poverty in the mid-1980s than there were in 1969. County level poverty data from North Carolina are informative here (Table 2.2). In the rural LMA counties of North Carolina, the rate of poverty increased by 22.8 percent between 1979 and 1983, and in 1983 there were 4.2 percent *more* people living in poverty in these counties than there were 14 years earlier. A similar pattern is also evident in the mid-size urban LMA counties. Even the black belt counties, which saw a mass out-migration of poor people during the 1960s and early 1970s, saw poverty rates begin to creep up again in the 1980s.

Table 2.2
Poverty Rates and Changes in the Number of Persons Living in Poverty in North Carolina: 1969-1983

	Urban		Rural	Black Belt
	Mid-Size	Small		
Poverty Rate (%)				
1969	17.1	21.8	19.4	36.8
1979	12.9	15.6	14.0	25.4
1983	14.6	18.0	16.6	27.4
Percent Change in the Number of Persons Living in Poverty				
1969-1979	-11.9	-17.5	-15.1	-29.6
1969-1983	3.3	-1.6	4.2	-23.1
1979-1983	17.3	19.3	22.8	9.2

Sources: North Carolina Poverty Estimates by County for Planning Purposes: 1979-1983. Raleigh, NC: State Data Center, Office of Budget and Management. U.S. Census of Population, 1970.

The rise in poverty rates across the South in the 1980s has not gone without notice. In 1986, the Southern Growth Policies Board commissioned a series of background papers dealing with critical cross-cutting issues facing the South. One of these papers was titled "Poverty in the South," by Steve Suitts of the Southern Regional Council in Atlanta. In this paper Suitts notes, "For the first time since the Great Depression we may be witnessing the growth of poverty and the formation of a real underclass of citizens while diminishing the government's efforts to assist the poor. It may also be an era when personal initiative and work become ineffective tools for many poor to escape their condition, when we assign a large and growing number of our children to live with poverty, and when the South returns to its worst tradition of ignoring the widening gap between the races."[5]

To reverse the trend toward increasing poverty and a growing divergence between the more affluent and less affluent groups in the region, Suitts calls for action at both the state and federal levels. His suggestions call for increasing the minimum wage and providing jobs for all poor adults who can work. (I will return to these points in the last chapter.) With respect to the minimum wage, Suitts observes that over one million poor people in the South could be lifted out of poverty if the minimum wage had been pegged to the inflation rate in recent years. Suitts also notes that full employment, at decent wages, is the most realistic way of eliminating poverty.[6]

Despite recent increases in poverty across all areas of the South in the 1980s, poverty rates in the rural and black belt LMAs have fallen considerably over the past 20 years, yet these areas have not been able to improve substantially their poverty standing vis-à-vis their more urban counterparts. This illustrates how economic development policies as they have been implemented in the past fall short of meeting the social justice criteria set forth by Rawls and others.[7] From a utilitarian perspective, of course, the decline in poverty across the LMAs justifies a continuation of past policies, since on the whole the situation has improved. However, from a non-utilitarian social justice position, the black belt and rural areas would have had to have shown a much greater improvement vis-à-vis the urban LMAs. By only keeping pace with the declining poverty rates in the urban LMAs and not closing the gap with these areas (Figure 2.1), the factors and conditions that have led to and perpetuated these structural inequalities remain unaddressed.

PER CAPITA INCOME

Low per capita income in the South both reflects and exacerbates the high rate of poverty in the region. Income is the most commonly used index of the well-being of an individual or a family in the United States. While per capita income is a very general measure of economic standing, it is an important and useful measure because the level of current income is related to the ability to purchase goods and services in the marketplace and the ability to choose among various life options.

The South has always lagged behind the other regions of the country in per capita income. In 1929, for example, the South's per capita income was only $362, or 52 percent of the national average. By 1946 the gap closed to 68 percent of the national average. And by 1979 southern per capita income was up to 92 percent of the national average. However, even today, there are only two southern states, Virginia and Florida, in which per capita income exceeds the national average. And in several states, notably Mississippi and South Carolina, there are no counties (rural or urban) in which per capita income equals the national average.

Several reasons have been put forth as explanations for the lagging per capita income in the South. Probably the most compelling explanation attributes the lag in per capita income to the region's insufficient rate of industrial growth. In a 1975 study of economic development in the South, Thomas Naylor and James Clotfelter argued that the insufficient industrialization that retarded economic growth in the region was the result of four "causal" factors. These four factors included: (1) an insufficient effective demand for goods and services in the region; 2) an insufficient supply of skilled and educated nonagricultural labor; 3) an insufficient supply of indigenous investment capital; and 4) an insufficient investment in education and technology.[8]

Within the South, the "causal" factors that impeded economic advancement were most evident in the more remote rural and black belt areas of the region. It is in these backwaters of the South where the largest concentrations of unskilled, poorly educated, agricultural workers reside. And the rural and black belt areas were the least able and least likely to invest in education and technology. Finally, because of the marginal nature of the farming enterprises that dominated the local economies of the rural and black belt areas, there was neither a large demand for manufactured goods and sophisticated services nor the ability to generate large quantities of investment capital.

Despite the fact that the South, especially the rural South, has historically lagged behind the nation as a whole in per capita income, the income gap had been steadily closing since at least the 1930s. In fact, the rapid growth of per capita income in the region vis-à-vis the rest of the nation, brought about in large measure by the collapse of the tenant/sharecropper system of agricultural production and mass out-migration of these displaced agricultural workers, led some observers in the 1960s, 1970s, and even the 1980s to predict that the South had a good chance of closing the gap entirely in the near future.[9] Unfortunately, the convergence in per capita income between many southern states, especially those in the Deep South, and the rest of the country appears to have come to an end in the late 1970s. Since that time a small, but unmistakable, regional *divergence* has been occurring. In Mississippi, for example, per capita income had risen to 71.0 percent of the national average by 1979. By 1986 it had slipped to 66.4 percent of the national average. During this same time span, Louisiana's per capita income fell from 88.1 percent of the national average to 76.4 percent, while Alabama's fell from 80.8 percent to 77.4 percent. In fact, with the exception of Virginia, Florida, North Carolina, and Georgia, which continued to close the per capita income gap, *all* other southern states lost ground between 1979 and 1986. Interestingly, the states with the largest rural populations were more likely to see their incomes diverge, while those with proportionately more urban residents were more likely to have experienced a convergence in recent years.

As with the data on poverty, per capita income data vary considerably across LMA groups in the South. The data reported in Figure 2.2 show that all LMA groups experienced a rise in per capita income between 1969 and 1983. Not surprisingly, the highest per capita income is found in the large urban LMA's while the rural and black belt LMA's have the lowest per capita income.

Despite impressive increases in per capita income in the rural and black belt LMAs between 1969 and 1983, the gap between these areas and the large urban LMAs actually grew larger (Table 2.3). In 1969, for instance, black belt per capita income was 59.9 percent of large urban per capita income. The gap in dollars was $3,269. By 1983, black belt per capita income had increased to 65.4 percent of the per capita income in the large urban LMAs. But the dollar gap

Figure 2.2
Per Capita Income by LMA Group: 1969-1983*

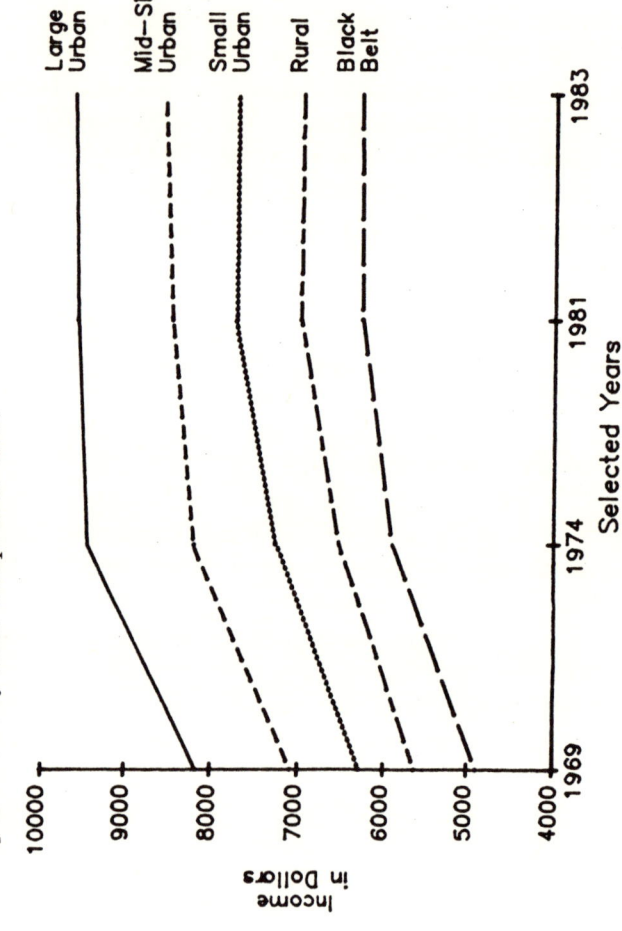

Source: U.S. County and City Data Book, various years.
*Income for all years is reported in 1983 dollars.

Table 2.3
Per Capita Income Comparisons: Black Belt and Rural LMAs as a Percentage of the Large Urban LMA and Differences Between the Large Urban LMA and the Black Belt and Rural LMAs *

Year	Black Belt & Large Urban (%)	Large – Black Urban – Belt ($)	Rural & Large Urban (%)	Large – Rural Urban ($)
1969	59.9	3269	68.9	2535
1974	62.5	3530	69.2	2907
1981	65.6	3281	73.0	2571
1983	65.4	3307	72.5	2627

Source: U.S. County and City Data Book, various years.

* Income for all years is reported in 1983 dollars.

had increased to $3,307. A similar pattern is also evident for the rural LMAs, where the ratio of rural to large urban per capita income increased from 68.9 percent in 1969 to 72.5 percent in 1983, but where the gap in personal income grew from $2,535 in 1969 to $2,627 in 1983. Furthermore, it is worth noting that for both the rural and black belt LMA groups, per capita income in 1983 was substantially lower than the 1969 per capita income in the large urban LMA groups.

What the data in Table 2.3 and Figure 2.2 illustrate is that inequalities among LMAs in the South have maintained themselves over time. Even with impressive relative increases in per capita income, the isolated rural and disadvantaged black belt LMAs have been unable to close the dollar gap with the more urban and prosperous LMAs in the South. With flattening income trajectories evident for all the LMA groups in recent years, the inequalities seem destined to remain for some time to come.

MANUFACTURING WAGES

Per capita income is usually considered a general measure of economic well-being for a population. It reflects all of the money derived from wages, salaries, transfer payments such as social security and retirement, interest income, and dividends. The largest component of per capita income in virtually all LMAs is wages and salaries. That is, money earned from a job. To better understand how and why per capita income varies across LMA groups it is helpful, then, to look at this key component.

Like per capita income, wages and salaries in the South generally, and in the rural South in particular, have historically lagged behind the national average.[10] One widely accepted explanation for the disparity in wage rates across rural and urban LMAs can be found in the product cycle model of regional economic growth. This model is based on three stages in a product's life cycle—innovation, growth, and standardization[11]—and is sometimes referred to as the "filtering-down" process of industrial development.[12]

The first phase of the product life cycle is characterized by a heavy emphasis on research and development activities. Well-educated, technologically sophisticated, and (not coincidentally) well-paid workers are found in industries that are on the cutting edge of product development. With few exceptions, plants engaged in innovative activities are found in large cities, since workers with the requisite scientific and engineering skills are typically concentrated in urban areas. The rural hinterlands cannot provide the talented workforces that these enterprises demand.[13]

The second phase of the product life cycle is one of product growth and market development. As product information spreads, new firms enter the marketplace. Intra-industry price competition heats up, which leads to a general shake-out of the less competitive firms in the industry. Management skills take on added importance in this phase as an increase in mergers and a tendency toward vertical integration also takes place in this phase. As with the activities in the innovative phase of the industry product cycle, most of the initial growth and mergers also takes place in urban locales.[14]

The third or "mature" phase in the product life cycle is one of standardization. By this time goods are manufactured in long production runs and few innovations of importance are introduced. It is at this point that wages become the key variable cost in the production process and it is also at this point that manufacturing enterprises no longer find a locational advantage in the cities. It is in the standardization phase that firms set up branch plants in rural areas where an abundant and non-unionized workforce is willing to work for comparatively low wages. It is also in this phase of the production cycle that many firms move their manufacturing operations to Third World locations.[15]

The data in Table 2.4 illustrate the wage disparities associated with the filtering down of industrial activity from urban centers to the rural hinterlands. Annual manufacturing wages are considerably higher in the urban LMAs in the South than in the rural or black belt LMAs. In 1982, for example, the black belt LMA with the *highest* average manufacturing wages ($14,953 for the LMA around Hinds County, Mississippi) ranked below the large urban LMA with the *lowest* average wages ($15,063) for the Miami–Fort Lauderdale, Florida, LMA. Furthermore, among the 36 rural LMAs, there was only one in which the average manufacturing wage exceeded the large urban LMA average.

In short, what we have in the South are distinctive sets of "high wage" and "low wage" LMAs. Large urban LMAs are consistently and overwhelmingly characterized by relatively high wages. Rural and black belt LMAs, on the other hand, are consistently and uni-

Table 2.4
Average Manufacturing Wages* by LMA Group: 1967, 1972, and 1982

	Urban			Rural	Black Belt
	Large	Mid-Size	Small		
1967 ($)	18,444	15,903	14,880	12,723	12,856
1972 ($)	19,886	17,524	16,246	14,156	13,772
1982 ($)	18,721	17,376	15,793	13,451	13,225

Source: Census of Manufacturing, 1967, 1972, 1982.

* Wages for all years are reported in 1982 dollars.

formly characterized by low wages. (I will have more to say about the nature and range of employment opportunities that give rise to these wage inequalities in Chapter 4.) It should also be noted here that the wage gap between the rural and black belt LMAs and the large urban LMAs had not closed at all between 1967 and 1982. The ratio of black belt manufacturing wages to large urban manufacturing wages has remained at about 0.70 since 1967. The same ratio holds for the manufacturing wages in rural LMAs compared to the wages in large urban LMAs.

While the rural and black belt LMAs made no headway in closing the wage gap with the large urban LMAs, they actually lost ground vis-à-vis the mid-size and small urban LMAs. That is, the gap between the rural and black belt LMAs and the mid-size and small urban LMAs actually increased. In 1972 manufacturing wages among the black belt LMAs was 78.3 percent of the mid-size LMA manufacturing wages. By 1982 this figure had fallen to 76.1 percent. Likewise, the ratio of rural LMA wages to mid-size urban LMA wages fell from 80.8 percent in 1972 to 77.4 percent in 1982.

Thus, on balance, patterns of industrial development in the South have maintained and in many instances exacerbated wage inequalities across LMA groups. Past industrial recruitment policies and programs were obviously successful in creating employment opportunities for workers in all LMAs of the South. The rural LMAs, for instance, experienced an 8.5 percent increase in manufacturing employment between 1972 and 1982, while the black belt LMAs showed a five percent increase in manufacturing jobs. Yet the fact remains that many rural and black belt LMAs have fallen further behind the larger and more urban places in the region. Clearly, until equity issues, especially as they pertain to wages, become part of the industrial recruitment agenda, we can probably expect these types of wage inequalities to persist.

WAGES IN OTHER INDUSTRIES

While the product cycle theory provides a plausible explanation for disparities in manufacturing wages across rural and urban labor markets, it is less directly useful in understanding wage differentials in other industries. Retail trade enterprises, which account for a large share of service sector employment, do not "filter down" in the same fashion as manufacturing enterprises from urban to rural locations in search of a low wage workforce. The same can be said for most other service industries. In fact, some service industries such as complex medical, legal, and financial services find locational advantage *only* in large metropolitan areas.

Rather than filtering down in a product cycle fashion, trade and service industries often follow in the wake of manufacturing industries to meet the needs generated by a growing manufacturing workforce. And, as might be expected, since the trade and service industries compete for labor in the same local labor market areas as manufacturing plants, they must pay their workers a wage that approximates prevailing wage levels in manufacturing. What this means for the rural and black belt LMAs, of course, is that trade and service industry wages will be considerably below those offered in the urban LMAs since manufacturing wage rates are lower outside of metropolitan areas.

To illustrate this phenomenon, I have selected wage and salary data for 1980 for the retail sales and professional services industries (Table 2.5). As expected, wage levels in both industries are lower in the black belt and rural LMAs than in the larger urban LMAs. In the retail trade industry, for example, the average wage level among the large urban LMAs was over 50 percent higher than in the rural and black belt LMAs. For the professional service industries, average large urban LMA wages were double those found in the black belt and

Table 2.5
Average Wages in the Retail Sales and Professional Service Industries in 1980, by LMA Group

	Urban			Rural	Black Belt
Industry	Large	Mid-Size	Small		
Retail Sales	15,022	13,461	10,863	9,893	10,900
Professional Service	18,496	13,526	10,781	8,511	8,864

Source: U.S. Census of Population, 1980.

rural LMAs. These latter figures, however, no doubt reflect the concentration of highly priced and specialized services (medical, legal, educational, financial) in the large urban areas of the region.

UNEMPLOYMENT AND UNDEREMPLOYMENT

Any discussion of wage rates and per capita income must be balanced with an examination of unemployment and underemployment levels. It should be readily apparent that relatively high wages mean very little to persons who cannot find work or who are employed in positions in which their talents and abilities are not fully compensated.

In the late 1970s and early 1980s, when the United States was mired in a period of high inflation coupled with economic stagnation, unemployment rates rose dramatically across the nation. While debate continues over exactly what level of unemployment constitutes "full employment," it is an undeniable fact that during the early 1980s millions of able-bodied Americans could not find work or were forced to accept either part-time jobs or positions for which they were overqualified. Despite the tremendous increase in the number of new jobs created in the South during this time, unemployment levels in both metropolitan and nonmetropolitan areas of the region were comparable, if not higher, to levels in other regions of the country.[16]

Within the South, the rural and black belt LMAs have historically experienced higher rates of unemployment than the more urban LMAs of the region. In the early 1970s, for example, when unemployment rates nationwide stood at about four percent, the black belt LMAs had an average unemployment rate of over five percent while the rural LMAs averaged over 4.5 percent unemployment (Table 2.6). In 1982, during the height of the recession, national unemployment soared to over nine percent. At this time the rural LMAs had an average unemployment rate of 11.7 percent and one out of every six rural LMAs had an unemployment rate in excess of 15 percent. Similarly, in 1982 the average black belt unemployment rate exceeded 12 percent.

As with the poverty, income, and wage data, divergence rather than convergence is evident in the unemployment data. Between 1970 and 1982 unemployment in the large urban LMAs went from 4.0 to 9.6 percent. The mid-size urban LMAs saw their unemploy-

Table 2.6
Average Unemployment Rates by LMA Group: 1970, 1980, 1982

	Urban			Rural	Black Belt
	Large	Mid-Size	Small		
1970 (%)	4.0	3.8	4.5	4.5	5.2
(N)	143,136	134,992	224,200	100,224	30,483
1980 (%)	6.0	5.7	7.0	7.3	7.7
(N)	307,240	298,352	484,685	226,836	57,420
1982 (%)	9.6	9.1	10.7	11.7	12.1
(N)	524,968	505,504	801,692	391,212	95,076

Source: U.S. Census of Population, 1970 and 1980, Bureau of Labor Statistics, 1982.

ment rate increase by 5.3 percent during this same period. In the rural LMAs, on the other hand, the unemployment rate went from 4.5 to 11.7 percent. The increase for the black belt LMAs was 6.9 percent. Thus, it is clear that not only are rural and black belt LMAs burdened with higher poverty rates and lower per capita income and wages than the more urban LMAs in the South, but they are also seeing their ranks of unemployed growing faster.

Part of the reason for the higher levels of unemployment in rural and black belt areas of the South can be attributed to changes in the structure of the region's agriculture and to the nonagricultural industry mix in these LMAs. Southern agriculture, more than any other region's agriculture, has been and remains dominated by small-scale, subsistence type farmers. These are farmers who are most vulnerable to changes in technology, to changes in markets, and to natural disasters such as floods, droughts, or killing frosts. Even after cotton production shifted out of the rural and black belt areas, these LMAs still maintained a large cadre of small producers. In 1969, for example, there were over 30,000 farmers in North Carolina with yearly farm sales of under $1,000. Alabama and Mississippi also had about 30,000 farmers in this category. By 1982, however, there were less than 10,000 farmers in each of these states in this category. Similar declines in the number of marginal producers were evident across the South. It seems reasonable to assume that many of these displaced individuals were not able to find off-farm employment and hence swelled the unemployment ranks.

Compounding the unemployment picture in the rural and black belt LMAs is a concentration of non-farm employment opportunities in low-wage manufacturing enterprises. As noted above, these are industries that are at the end of the product cycle and who now seek out economic backwaters where wages are low. Beginning in the late 1970s and continuing today, many of the industries that once found a haven in the rural South have begun to move their operations to Third World countries, where wages are even lower and workers less organized than in the rural and black belt LMAs. What this means, then, is that not only has the growth of branch plants slowed in recent years, but many existing enterprises have shut down. Not surprisingly, given a scenario of rural deindustrialization, unemployment rates in the rural and black belt LMAs have risen.

Urban areas, of course, have not been immune to the ravages of unemployment. In fact, in terms of absolute numbers, the three urban LMA groups added over one million persons to the unemployment rolls between 1970 and 1982. At the same time that the number of unemployed was rising, however, the more urban LMAs were generating millions of new jobs. In other words, the emerging divergence in unemployment rates between rural and black belt LMAs, on the one hand, and the urban LMAs on the other, has as much to do with job creation as with job disappearance. Simply stated, urban LMAs have been more successful than rural and black belt LMAs in creating jobs.

Underemployment is a more difficult concept to measure since no government agency at the state or federal level collects or disseminates this type of information. Several independent studies by economists and sociologists, however, using different estimation techniques and relying on different types of data, have consistently shown that underemployment is more of a problem in rural areas than in urban places, and more prevalent in the South than elsewhere.[17] For the illustrative purposes of this chapter, I have chosen to operationalize "underemployment" as the proportion of the population aged 18–64 that is not in the labor force. Phrased differently, the degree of underemployment in a population can be measured by dividing the active labor force, those currently employed or seeking work, by the total potential labor force (i.e., all persons aged 18–64). This is sometimes referred to as the labor force participation rate and is an admittedly crude proxy of underemployment since it includes persons who are not really "underemployed" at all, such as college students. It also includes persons who are unable, because of physical or mental disability, to hold a job. Furthermore, it excludes persons who are working, but who are clearly over-qualified for the work they are doing. Nevertheless, by assuming that the proportions of the population in each LMA that are mistakenly included or excluded in the computations are roughly equal, then this measure of underemployment has some degree of validity.

The results presented in Table 2.7 confirm what other studies have shown, namely that "underemployment" rates are higher in rural areas than they are in urban locales. In the black belt and rural LMAs, over 27 percent of the 18–64 population was not in the labor force. In the large and mid-size urban LMAs, on the other hand, only 24.1 percent and 22.9 percent, respectively, were not in the labor force. What is also apparent in Table 2.7 is that between 1970 and 1980 underemployment decreased across all LMA groups, but the decrease was greatest in the mid-size urban category and least in the black belt category. Thus, here is one more instance where divergence rather than convergence between the rural and urban South is occurring.

Table 2.7
Average Underemployment Rate by LMA Group: 1970 and 1980

| | Urban | | | | |
	Large	Mid-Size	Small	Rural	Black Belt
1970 (%)	28.6	27.9	30.6	32.2	31.2
1980 (%)	24.1	22.9	26.3	27.4	27.8
Δ (%)	4.5	5.0	4.3	4.8	3.4

Source: U.S. Censuses of Population, 1970 and 1980.

There are at least two possible explanations for the higher level of underemployment in the rural and black belt LMAs and the growing divergence between these places and the more highly urbanized LMAs. First, workers living outside of metropolitan labor markets typically confront a more restricted set of occupational opportunities than their more urban counterparts, and consequently it is more likely that they would be unable to find a job that matched their talents and interests. As a result, a larger share of the rural labor supply is likely to drop out of the labor force in these LMAs.

Second, many rural and black belt LMAs have historically lagged behind the urban LMAs in employment growth. This means that labor turnover and the chances for occupational mobility (i.e., the opportunity to change jobs) are lower in the less urbanized LMAs in the South. It is possible that workers in these areas become more easily discouraged with finding a job and simply stop looking for work.

CONCLUSIONS

What I have attempted to show in this chapter is that regardless of the measure of economic well-being, one cannot escape the conclusion that the rural and black belt labor market areas of the South have remained relatively poorer and more underdeveloped vis-à-vis their more urban counterparts. The measures I selected to illustrate the plight of persons living in rural and black belt LMAs were designed to tap a broad and diverse range of factors that social scientists have shown to be related to the quality of life and standard of living in an area. The data presented in this chapter clearly show that poverty rates are higher, per capita income and wages are lower, and unemployment and underemployment is more prevalent outside of the urban LMAs of the region. More distressing, perhaps, is the fact that in many instances there appears to be a growing divergence between the relatively affluent urban LMAs in the South and the economically distressed rural and black belt LMAs on these dimensions. In virtually no instance have the rural and black belt LMAs made substantial strides in closing the gap with the urban LMAs of the region.

Taking the long view of economic changes in the South, it is undeniable that the quality of life and standard of living in the more isolated and predominantly black areas of the region have improved considerably over the past 25 years. Poverty rates did come down, per capita income increased, and underemployment decreased. Several observers remain optimistic that additional improvements lie ahead. They view the economic stagnation and the growing disparities between rural and urban LMAs that I have begun to articulate in this chapter as merely a brief dip in an otherwise upward trajectory.

Others, however, are not so sanguine about the ability of the rural and black belt South to make further in-roads in closing the economic gap with the rest of the country. They believe that these areas have come about as far as they can and have little chance of making up any more ground. Georgia State Representative Pete Phillips recently acknowledged the growing gulf between the rural and urban areas in his state when he said, "We live in two Georgias. We live in an urban Georgia that is booming, prospering, creating new jobs and opportunities. We live in a rural Georgia that is on the decline and losing jobs, people and confidence."[18] In short, a "rural crisis" has swept over the region in the mid-1980s. The simultaneous decline of both agriculture and manufacturing has undermined local economies, displaced workers, and created a growing underclass.

Compounding these problems, during the 1980s federal support for rural development activities declined. The Office of Rural Development Planning, for instance, was abolished in 1986 as a result of budget cuts. As a recent Ford Foundation report, *Shadows in the Sunbelt*, noted: "Expensive as these programs have been, they have proven valuable to the rural South—helping to provide the training and technical assistance, start-up capital and, most important, infrastructure necessary for economic development."[19] In lieu of federal support for rural development, state and local development officials were told to pick themselves up by their own bootstraps and to seek new and novel strategies to promote employment and economic growth. As the Ford Foundation report put it: "The key to alternative development strategies lies in public entrepreneurship provided by local organizations."[20]

State and local governments have attempted to rise to the challenge by developing and instituting a new set of de facto industrial policies. Several southern states including Mississippi, South Carolina, and Arkansas have increased funding for education. Other states are establishing incubator facilities to encourage small business growth. There is little evidence, however, that these efforts will be any more successful in raising the standard of living and quality of life of rural and black belt residents than past efforts have been.

From an economic justice perspective, the longstanding inequalities between rural and black belt LMAs on the one hand, and the more urban LMAs on the other, on virtually all quality of life measures, and the emerging divergence on many of these measures evident since the late 1970s, suggests a radical rethinking of the role of past economic development programs and policies is necessary. The disadvantageous economic conditions in the rural and black belt areas of the South are destined to remain unchanged until the country as a whole dedicates itself to alleviating these problems. Short-term, locally devised and administered de facto policies have worked mainly to exacerbate the differences that already exist. The more prosperous and affluent urban labor markets are generally better able to provide a context conducive to growth and development. Rural and black belt areas simply do not have the human resources or necessary infrastructure to compete against these areas for economic development. And without a strong federal presence, these less advantaged places seem destined to fall further behind.

NOTES

1. Briggs Jr., Vernon M., Brian S. Rungeling, and Lewis H. Smith, 1978. *Human Needs and Income Supplement Programs in the Rural South* (Center for Manpower Studies, University of Mississippi), p. 3.

2. The President's National Advisory Commission on Rural Poverty, 1967, *The People Left Behind* (Washington, D.C.: U.S. Government Printing Office), p. ix.

3. Ibid.

4. Auchmutey, Jim, and Priscilla Painton, 1986, "Rural Refugees Tote Their Troubles into Southern Cities," *Atlanta Constitution* (November 20).

5. Suitts, Steve, 1986, "Poverty in the South," in Lucy R. Watkins (ed.), *Equity: The Critical Link in Southern Economic Development* (Research Triangle Park, NC: Southern Growth Policies Board), pp. 21-24.

6. Ibid.

7. Rawls, John, 1971. *A Theory of Justice* (Cambridge, MA: Harvard University Press).

8. Naylor, Thomas H., and James Clotfelter, 1975, *Strategies for Change in the South* (Chapel Hill: University of North Carolina Press).

9. For a recent example of this type of forecasting, see Thomas E. James Jr., "Anticipating Future Growth in the Sunbelt," in Steven C. Ballard and Thomas E. James (eds.), *The Future of the Sunbelt* (New York: Praeger Publishers, 1983), pp. 37-62.

10. See, for example, Frank A. Hanna, 1959, *State Income Differentials 1919-1954* (Durham, NC: Duke University Press). Also see, "50 Year Trend Reversed as U.S. Regions Grow Apart Economically," *New York Times* (August 23, 1987), p. 18.

11. Kale, Steven R., 1986, "Stability, Growth, and Adaptability to Economic and Social Change in Rural Labor Markets," in Molly S. Killian, Leonard E. Bloomquist, Shelley Pendelton, and David McGranahan (eds.), *Symposium on Rural Labor Markets Research Issues*, Economic Research Service, U.S. Department of Agriculture Staff Report AGES860721 (Washington, D.C.: U.S. Government Printing Office).

12. Thompson, Wilbur, 1965, *A Preface to Urban Economics* (Baltimore: The Johns Hopkins Press).

13. Ibid.

14. Ibid.

15. Ibid.

16. Bluestone, Herman, and John Hession, 1986, "Patterns of Change in the Nonmetro and Metro Labor Force since 1979," in D. Jahr, J. Johnson, and R. Wimberely (eds.), *New Dimensions in Rural Policy: Building Upon Our Heritage*, Joint Economic Committee of the U.S. Congress (Washington, D.C.: U.S. Government Printing Office), pp. 121-33.

17. See, for example, Peter F. Korsching and Stephen G. Sapp, 1978, "Unemployment Estimation in Rural Areas: A Critique of Official Procedures and a Comparison with Survey Data," *Rural Sociology* 43 (Spring), pp. 101-110. Also see, Daniel T. Lichter and Janice A. Costanzo, 1986, "Underemployment in Nonmetropolitan America, 1970-1982," in Jahr, Johnson, and Wimberely (eds.), *New Dimensions in Rural Policy*, pp. 134-43; and Daniel T. Lichter, 1988, "Race and Underemployment: Black Employment Hardship in the South," in L. J. Beaulieu (ed.), *The Rural South in Crisis* (Boulder, CO: Westview), pp. 181-97.

18. Quoted in William E. Schmidt, "Not All of the South is in the Sunbelt," *New York Times* (January 19, 1986).

19. *Shadows in the Sunbelt*, A Report of the MDC Panel on Rural Economic Development, May 1986 (Chapel Hill: MDC, Inc.).

20. Ibid.

3. Health, Education, and Welfare: Creating and Sustaining Human Capital in the South

> The Commission recommends that the United States adopt and put into effect immediately a national policy designed to give the residents of rural America equality of opportunity with all other citizens. This must include equal access to ... medical care, housing, education, welfare, and all other public services. ...[1]

Human resource development is a term that was popularized by policymakers and program planners in the 1960s. In its broadest sense, it connotes a concerted effort on the part of federal, state, and local governments, in cooperation with the private sector, to upgrade the quality and skill level of the workforce. Human resource development programs and activities in places like the rural South are essential parts of any industrial policy agenda. They rest on the assumption that local labor markets saddled with low-skilled, poorly educated, and less healthy workers are not likely to attract and keep high paying, stable employment opportunities.

Put quite simply, the policies and infrastructure that are put into place to foster human resource development will, in the end, create and sustain human capital in an area. In this chapter, I examine three aspects of human resource development: education and schools, healthcare, and welfare. My purpose is to see how the less affluent rural and black belt areas of the South compare with the more prosperous urban areas of the region in their ability to meet the human resource development needs of their residents.

Historically, the South has lagged behind other regions of the country not only on economic measures such as per capita income, poverty, and the like, but also on measures of human capital development and social welfare. The educational standing of the adult population, which is the most widely used indicator of the stock of human capital in an area, is a good case in point. In 1960 only 35.3 percent of the adults in the South had graduated from high school and only 7.1 percent held college degrees. Nationally, in 1960, 41.1 percent of the adult population had graduated from high school and 7.7 percent were college graduates. Viewed a bit differently, in 1960 only Florida ranked above the national average in the percentage of high school graduates and only Florida and Virginia ranked above the national average in the percentage of college graduates.

By 1980 the percentage of high school graduates in the South had risen to 60.2 percent and the percentage of college graduates had grown to 14.8 percent. Yet the South still trailed all other regions on these measures. In the United States as a whole, 66.5 percent of the adults in 1980 were high school graduates and 16.3 percent had college degrees. Again, by 1980 only Florida had more high school graduates than the national average and only Virginia had a higher percentage of college graduates.

In this same vein, per capita expenditures for schooling have been and remain lower in the South than in any other region. Even today, there is only one southern state (Florida) in which per capita spending for public education equals the national average. In many states, spending not only remains appallingly low, but is falling further behind the national average. In Mississippi, for instance, per-pupil expenditures in 1974 stood at $899. This was 69.9 percent of the national average of $1,286. By 1984, Mississippi's expenditures of $1,962 had fallen to only 61.8 percent of the national average of $3,173. Likewise, in Alabama per pupil expenditures in 1974 were 71 percent of the national average, but had fallen to 66.2 percent by 1984, while South Carolina fell from 81.1 to 71.1 percent during this same period.[2]

The South has also trailed the rest of the country on social welfare measures such as health and medical care. Infant mortality rates, for example, have always exceeded the national average. The South has the lowest per capita number of doctors, dentists, and hospitals. It has the highest rate of out-of-wedlock births and teenage mothers, and life expectancy is lower in the South than elsewhere.[3]

Overall, of course, in line with the trends in per capita income and poverty, the South has made impressive strides over the past 25 years in efforts to upgrade education, healthcare, and social services for its residents. However, much of the gain stems from the relatively lowly position of the South to begin with. Furthermore, the gains the South has made have varied from place to place across the region. As the data presented in this chapter will demonstrate, the more urban areas of the sunbelt have clearly outdistanced the black belt and rural LMAs in improving human capital and social welfare conditions in the region.

EDUCATIONAL ATTAINMENT, SCHOOL FUNDING, AND TEACHER QUALITY

Improving the quality of public schools and subsequently enhancing the educational standing of the southern labor force has become the avowed goal of virtually every governor and state legislature in the region. Without a literate and skilled workforce, they know that the South has little chance of attracting or generating high paying employment opportunities. In recent years almost all of the southern states have taken concrete steps to improve their school systems. South Carolina and Mississippi dedicated a one cent sales tax hike to education in the mid-1980s. Other states have raised teachers' salaries and instituted standardized competency tests for both students and teachers.[4]

This recent flurry of state-level activity must be put into a broader perspective, however. Despite the programs and policies espoused and put into place by governors and state legislatures and the additional federal and state funding that has been pumped into local school districts across the region, the local community still exercises tremendous influence and control over the educational enterprise. Funding for special programs, building and maintaining school facilities, and the hiring (and firing) of teachers are some of the activities that fall within the purview of local school superintendents and/or local school boards. Property tax revenues are generally a key source of local educational funding. The ability of a community to enhance educational quality rests, in part at least, on the willingness of local leaders to support these types of revenues. Generally speaking, more prosperous and urban areas are able to provide the resources necessary to sustain a quality system of education, and this commitment to education is reflected in the educational credentials of their residents.

The large and mid-size urban LMAs, for example, contain proportionately more college graduates than the rural and black belt LMAs (Table 3.1). In 1980, over one in seven adults living in the large or mid-size urban LMAs had a college degree. Among the rural LMA residents, less than one in ten had a college degree in 1980. In fact, in six of the 36 rural LMAs in the South, less than one person in 15 was a college graduate.

Consistent with national trends, all of the LMA groups in the South experienced increases in the number of college graduates between 1970 and 1980, and presumably are continuing to see the number of college graduates rise in the 1980s. However, the increase has been greatest in the large urban LMAs (117.1 percent) and smallest in the more rural black belt LMAs (85.4 percent). Thus, even though the black belt LMAs are increasing their stock of human capital (i.e., college graduates), they are doing it at a rate that will cause them to fall further behind the more urban LMAs in the region.

Race differences are also reported in Table 3.1. It is clear from these data that whites are considerably more likely to hold college degrees compared with nonwhites, across the LMA types. Perhaps the most interesting finding in Table 3.1, however, is the comparatively high percentage of college educated whites in the black belt LMAs. In 1980, over 14 percent of all black belt whites were college graduates while less than seven percent of the nonwhites in the black belt had graduated from college. This large racial gap in educational attainment clearly shows that the pool of well-educated manpower is disproportionately concentrated among the white population. More importantly, these results suggest that, all other things being equal, white workers are probably in a better position than black workers to take advantage of those job opportunities that favor brain over brawn.

This latter point is reinforced by the finding in Panel B of Table 3.1. Almost half of all adult blacks living in the black belt in 1980 had less than a ninth grade education. On the other hand, less than one-fifth of the whites in the black belt had failed to complete at least nine years of schooling. This disparity is important when one realizes that many government and business officials consider a ninth grade education to represent minimum literacy. Persons with less than a ninth grade education are assumed to be, in many instances,

Table 3.1
Educational Characteristics of People Over 25 Years Old by LMA Group

	Urban			Rural	Black Belt
	Large	Mid-Size	Small		
A) College Graduates					
Total 1970%	10.0	9.7	7.7	6.1	7.2
Total 1980%	15.4	15.0	11.5	9.6	10.8
1970-1980 Δ%	117.1	106.3	94.0	105.8	85.4
Whites 1980%	17.2	16.7	12.8	10.2	14.1
Blacks 1980%	8.8	9.4	6.8	6.4	6.6
B) Less Than Nine Years of Schooling					
Whites 1980%	16.0	18.6	23.5	31.1	19.9
Blacks 1980%	31.1	31.9	38.2	40.7	48.8
Total 1980%	19.0	21.9	26.8	33.1	32.4
C) Percent of the School Age Population (Ages 14-18) Not in School					
Whites 1980%	15.6	16.4	17.9	19.2	14.6
Blacks 1980%	15.4	15.4	15.7	15.0	15.7
Total 1980%	15.5	16.1	17.3	18.4	15.2

Sources: U.S. Census of Population, 1980.

functionally illiterate and suitable for only the most low skilled and menial jobs.

Although whites living in the black belt compare favorably with their more urban counterparts, the same cannot be said for whites who reside in the rural LMAs. Almost one-third of these individuals had failed to complete the ninth grade, while only about one in ten was a college graduate. In five of the rural LMAs, over 40 percent of the whites had less than a ninth grade education.

Compounding these problems is the comparatively high drop-out rate in the rural LMAs (Panel C, Table 3.1). In 1980, almost one in five white youths in the rural areas between the ages of 14 and 18 had dropped out of school without receiving a high school diploma. Given this lack of commitment to formal education by rural young people, it is likely that the stock of human capital in these LMAs will remain far below that found in the more urban LMAs of the region. And in the quest for high wage, high skill jobs, the poor educational standing of the workforce in the rural LMAs will surely be a detriment.

There are various other ways that could be used to document the gaps in educational credentials among residents of the black belt and rural LMAs and those living in the more urban LMAs in the South. However, the data in Table 3.1 make the point clearly enough. Inequalities in educational achievement exist and persist among the various LMA groups (and across racial groups within the LMAs) and in many instances these inequalities have been growing larger in recent years.

The inability of the rural and black belt areas of the South to enhance the educational standing of their residents vis-à-vis the more urban places of the region rests, in part, on the meager local tax base that can be drawn upon to support public education. When a locality offers a tax holiday to a prospective employer, it means that it is gutting its ability to meet key social welfare needs, including education. The data in Panel A of Table 3.2 show that per capita property taxes have historically been the lowest in the rural and black belt LMAs and the highest in the large urban LMAs. In fact, in 1982 the average rural LMA per capita property tax ($142) was nearly half that of the large urban LMA average ($249), while the average black belt per capita property tax ($144) was only slightly higher than that found among the rural LMAs.

When local property taxes are reported as a percentage of total educational expenditures, it is obvious that urban areas, especially the large and mid-size urban LMAs are in a much more favorable position to support a broader range of public services than the smaller and more rural LMAs. Local property taxes represent about 65 percent of expenditures for public education in the large urban LMAs. In the rural and black belt LMAs they account for only about 35 percent. Furthermore, between 1977 and 1982, the ratio between property taxes and school expenditures dropped only slightly in the large urban LMAs, but this ratio registered a more substantial drop in the rural and especially black belt LMAs.

Interestingly, between 1977 and 1982, property taxes (in real dollars) decreased in all LMA groups in the South. The decrease was smallest, however, among the large urban LMAs (2.0 percent). On the other hand, property taxes fell substantially in the rural and black belt areas. Among the rural LMAs, the average decline in property taxes was 5.7 percent while they fell by 6.5 percent in the black belt.

Despite the fact that the rural and black belt areas saw property tax revenues decline, overall per pupil funding in the rural and black belt LMAs did not fall and, in fact, the level of per-pupil funding compares favorably with the urban areas of the region. What this means, of course, is that state and federal sources have been used to supplement declines in local revenues. In principle, nonlocal financial aid to schools is desirable since it serves to equalize funding among local school districts. Certainly, impoverished areas of the South need this type of support if they are to make any meaningful educational improvements. However, by relying more and more on nonlocal sources, it means that when various states or the federal government are forced to cut spending, funding for local schools is jeopardized. And the greater the dependency on nonlocal sources, the greater the vulnerability.[5]

Although the poorer areas of the South will be dependent on outside assistance for some time to come, it makes little sense to use this outside aid as an excuse to cut local taxes, especially when one considers that per capita income has not dropped (see Table 2.3). However, it appears in Table 3.2 that rural and black belt areas are doing just that. They seem content simply to substitute federal and state dollars for local dollars and in the process fall further behind the larger urban areas in the region.

Part of the reason why local funding for public education in the black belt remains so low is tied to the issue of race. After the federal

Table 3.2
Funding and Expenditures for Public Schooling in the South and Distribution of Enrollment by School Type

	Urban			Rural	Black Belt
	Large	Mid-Size	Small		
A) Per Capita Property Taxes 1982 ($)	249	202	169	142	144
Property Taxes as a Percent of Educational Expenditures					
1977 (%)	65.7	51.0	42.4	38.8	37.7
1982 (%)	64.4	48.8	39.7	36.4	34.5
Percent Change in Property Taxes 1977-1982	-2.0	-4.3	-5.4	-5.7	-6.5

B) School Type: 1980

White Students				
Public	81.3	89.2	91.1	95.9	77.1
Church-Related	14.8	7.4	6.0	2.6	6.9
Private	3.9	3.4	2.9	1.5	16.0
Total (%)	100.0	100.0	100.0	100.0	100.0
Black Students				
Public	94.7	97.8	97.5	99.0	97.8
Church-Related	4.2	1.7	2.0	.5	1.9
Private	1.1	.5	.5	.5	.3
Total (%)	100.0	100.0	100.0	100.0	100.0

Sources: COSTAT II and U.S. Census of Population, 1980.

courts mandated that the South could no longer maintain segregated schools, there was a mass exodus of whites out of the public school system. A network of private segregation academies sprang up almost overnight across the region. Although some of these academies have a religious affiliation and have justified their existence on religious grounds, many are independent entities designed solely to keep black and white students apart. As the data in Panel B of Table 3.2 show, nearly one of every four white children living in the black belt in 1980 attended some type of private school. Only about one in fifty black children attended a private school in the black belt in 1980.

Although remarkably little is known about how these segregation academies are run, it is apparent that they have siphoned off the upper and middle class children from the public schools. In doing this, they have served to undercut sentiment among many whites to raise taxes to improve public education. Given this conundrum, it is unlikely that public education can appreciably improve in the black belt without large subsidies of state and federal monies.

One other set of statistics illustrates the educational problems of the rural and black belt South. These data deal with the qualifications and salaries of schoolteachers. Studies have shown that teachers can make a difference in raising the achievement and aspiration levels of students.[6] However, the law of supply and demand dictates that the best qualified teachers will be likely to go where the salaries are highest. In the South, teacher salaries are highest in the urban LMAs.

In 1980, schoolteachers in the large urban LMAs earned on average $9,351 a year (Figure 3.1). This was 10.7 percent more than teachers in the rural LMAs received and 8.7 percent more than teachers in the black belt made. Not coincidentally, teachers in the large urban LMAs have better educational credentials than those in the other LMA groups. Nearly 45 percent had pursued at least some formal training beyond the bachelor degree. In the other LMA groups, on the other hand, only between 38.0 and 40.5 percent of the teachers had sought additional education beyond the bachelor degree.

HEALTHCARE AND DELIVERY

Over twenty years ago, the President's National Advisory Commission on Rural Poverty noted the lack of modern health services and

Figure 3.1
Characteristics of Teachers in the South

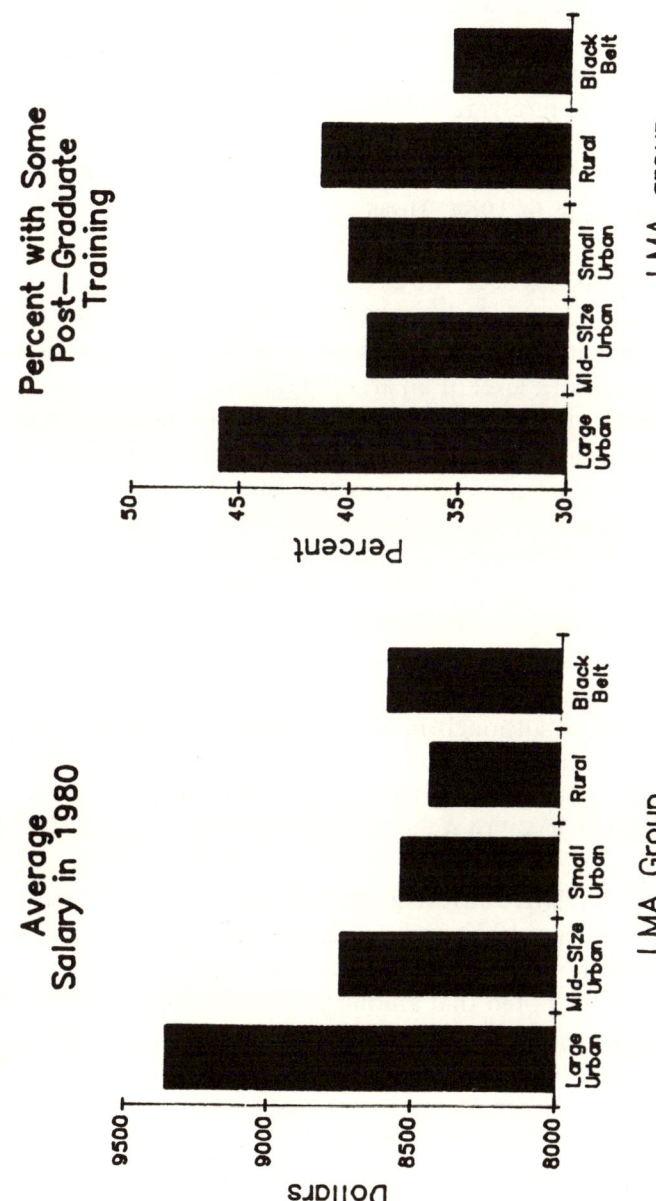

Source: 1980 Census of Population.

the low standards of medical and dental care in rural America, generally, and in the rural South in particular. The authors of that report stated that the healthcare in the rural South was "... not only inadequate in extent, but seriously deficient in quality. It is badly organized, underfinanced, rarely related to the needs of the individual or the family."[7]

Admittedly, the situation has improved since that harsh assessment was made in 1964. However, the inequities between the rural and the urban South that were documented in the President's Report still persist. As has been the case in so many other instances, many of these inequities seem to have grown larger in recent years. We can use infant mortality, which reflects social and economic conditions and the general health level of an area, to illustrate this point.

The data in Table 3.3 reveal that the infant mortality rate has continued to decline across all LMAs in the South. However, the infant death rate has been and remains consistently higher in the black belt LMAs than in the other LMA groups. Furthermore, the infant mortality rate for blacks living in the black belt has been higher than the infant mortality rate for blacks outside of the black belt. In fact, the infant mortality rate for blacks living in the black belt in 1982 was higher than the infant mortality rate for any groups of whites in 1970.

Interestingly, although infant deaths have declined for both blacks and whites, the relative difference between races is largest in the black belt and is growing larger. The infant death rate for blacks in the black belt was 114.4 percent higher than whites in 1970 but rose to 130.6 percent higher by 1982. Three of the other LMA groups also saw the relative difference between black and white infant deaths increase between 1970 and 1982. However, in none of these cases was the difference as large as in the black belt.

It should be noted that among whites, the highest infant mortality rates are found among the rural LMAs. In both 1970 and 1982, the white infant death rate exceeded the rates in the other LMAs. In short, despite rather dramatic progress in decreasing infant deaths in the more isolated and low income areas of the South, these areas still lag behind the more urban areas of the region and there is little indication that the gaps will ever close completely.

Related to this, at the bottom of Table 3.3, the percentage of babies classified as having a "low birth weight" is reported. This is an important statistic because low birth weight babies are at risk vis-à-vis

Table 3.3
Infant Mortality Rates and Low Birth Weight Babies by LMA Group

	Urban			Rural	Black Belt
	Large	Mid-Size	Small		
Infant Mortality (Per 1000 live births)					
1970 Total	21.3	22.3	22.7	23.8	29.3
White	17.4	18.3	18.0	21.2	17.4
Black	31.1	32.8	35.1	36.3	38.3
Black + White (%)	78.7	79.2	95.0	71.2	114.4
1982 Total	12.9	13.4	13.0	12.2	16.5
White	9.8	10.3	10.2	10.8	9.4
Black	19.7	20.6	19.9	19.4	21.4
Black + White (%)	101.0	100.0	95.1	79.6	130.6
% of All Babies With Low Birth Weight	8.2	8.0	7.8	7.3	9.5

Source: Area Resource File, 1985.

illness and disease during the first year of life. Consistent with the infant mortality data, the black belt LMAs have a greater proportion of low birth weight babies than the other LMA groups. In fact, in three of the nine black belt LMAs, over one in ten births produces a low birth weight baby. By way of comparison, among the 83 separate LMAs that make up the large, mid-size, and small urban LMA groups, only three had a rate in excess of 10 percent.

Another indicant of general social welfare is the percentage of children born to teenage mothers (Figure 3.2). Research has shown that although the negative effects of maternal age on pregnancy and neonatal health are largely mediated by the quality of healthcare in an area, the children of teenage mothers are more likely to experi-

Figure 3.2
Percentage of Children Born to Teenage Mothers by LMA Group, 1978–1982

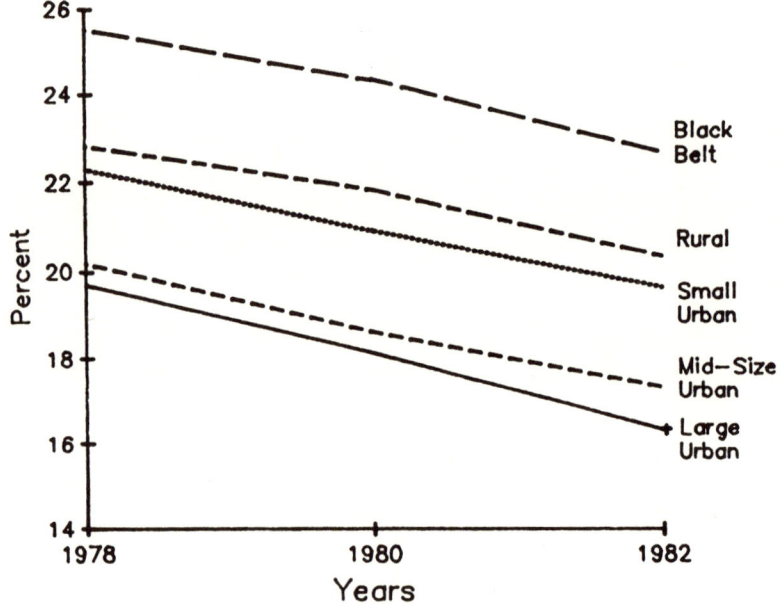

Source: Area Resource File, 1985.

ence problems in their physical, cognitive, and social development. Additional findings indicate that teenage parents are least able to support a family and most likely to end up on welfare after the child is born.[8]

As was the case with infant mortality, there has been an overall decline in the number of children born to teenagers in the LMAs. The percentage is lowest in the urban LMAs in the region and highest in the rural and black belt LMAs. Furthermore, the drop in the percentage of children born to teenage mothers has been greatest in the large urban LMAs (3.5 percent) and smallest in the rural LMAs (2.5 percent), and the relative difference between the urban LMAs and the rural and black belt LMAs is growing larger. In 1978, the percentage of children born to mothers under 20 years old who lived in rural LMAs was 16.6 percent higher than that for teenagers living in large urban LMAs. It was 29.4 percent higher for mothers living in the black belt LMAs. By 1982, the differences had grown to 25.3 percent for rural LMAs and 39.5 percent for black belt LMAs.

These differences in health measures among the five LMA groups and especially between the urban LMAs and the rural and black belt LMAs are exacerbated by the scarcity of healthcare manpower and facilities in the more isolated areas of the South. The location of Health Maintenance Organizations (HMOs) across the region illustrates this point. HMOs are a relatively new method for healthcare delivery. They have two fundamental attributes that distinguish them from traditional healthcare delivery systems. First, they bring together a comprehensive range of medical services in a single organization so that a patient is assured of ready access to all of them. And second, HMOs provide these services for a fixed contract fee that is paid in advance by all subscribers. It has been noted that HMOs yield lower hospital use, relatively more preventative services, and lower overall costs to the patient than conventional open market, fee-for-service healthcare.[9]

In 1982, there were no HMOs in any of the black belt LMAs and only one rural LMA had an HMO. In contrast, all of the large urban LMAs had at least one HMO by 1982 and many had several. Likewise, all but four of the 16 mid-size urban LMAs had at least one HMO.

The presence or absence of an HMO, of course, is no guarantee that healthcare will be readily available at a reasonable cost to all residents of an area. However, the fact that the number of HMOs is growing rapidly in the urban LMAs of the South, and that they are virtually nonexistent in the rural and black belt areas, suggests that this innovative and cost-effective means of healthcare delivery is being denied to a large segment of the region's population, a segment that in many ways is most in need of this type of service.

Compounding and contributing to the healthcare problems confronting rural and black belt residents is a striking dearth of physicians and dentists. In 1983 the large urban LMAs averaged one physician for every 486 residents (Figure 3.3). In the rural LMAs, on the other hand, there was one physician for every 1220 residents in 1983. Among the black belt LMAs, the average physician-to-resident ratio was 1 to 1235. And only one of the nine black belt LMAs had a population-to-physician ratio of less than 1000 to 1.

Although the ratio of residents to physicians has been falling in all of the LMA groups, it has fallen most dramatically in the urban LMAs and has fallen the least in the rural and black belt LMAs. In the large and mid-size urban LMAs, for instance, the population-to-physician ratio dropped by 44 percent between 1960 and 1983, while in the small urban LMAs it declined by 40 percent. Among the rural and black belt LMAs, the percentage fell by only 28.1 and 31.8 percent, respectively, during the same period. Looked at a bit differently, the rural and black belt LMAs are lagging more than 25 years behind the more urban areas of the region in the population-to-physician ratio. That is, in 1960, the large and mid-size urban LMAs had more physicians per 100,000 population than the rural and black belt areas have today.

The patterns are similar for dentists (Table 3.4). There are considerably more dentists in the urban areas of the South than in the rural hinterlands. In 1981, for example, in the large and mid-size urban LMAs, there was one dentist for every 2000 residents. In the same year in the rural and black belt LMAs, there was one dentist for every 3300–3800 residents.

Other research has shown that physicians and dentists are not the only healthcare workers who are disproportionately concentrated in urban areas of the South. There are about 60 percent more nurses per capita in metropolitan than in nonmetropolitan areas of the South. Likewise allied health professionals such as speech and language pathologists, physical, respiratory, and occupational therapists, and dental hygienists are more readily available in urban areas of the region. A recent study in Georgia, for example, found that metro-

Figure 3.3
Physician-to-Population Ratio by LMA Group (1960–1983)

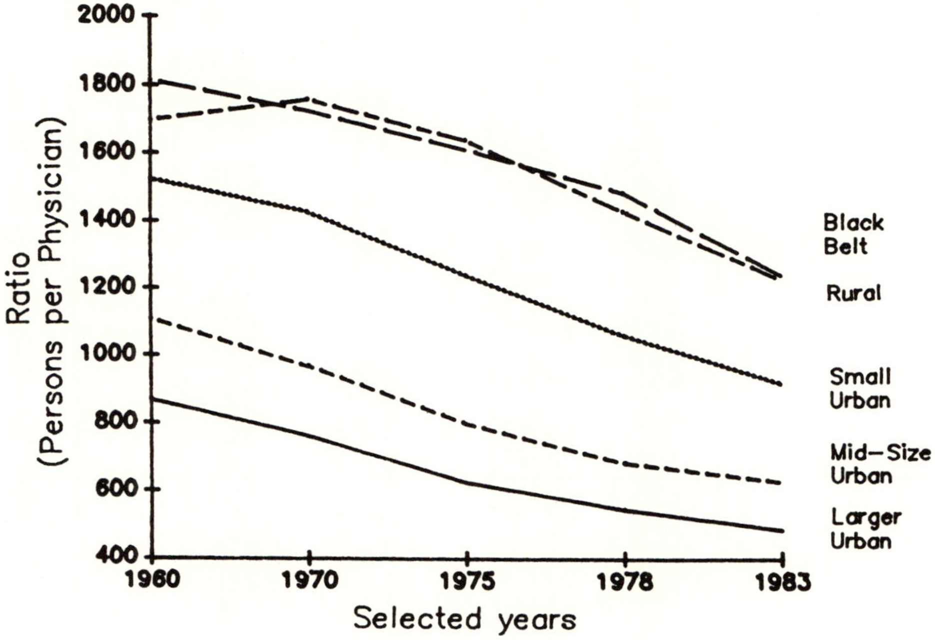

Source: Area Resource File, 1985.

Table 3.4
Dentist-to-Population Ratio 1976–1981 by LMA Group

	Urban			Rural	Black Belt
	Large	Mid-Size	Small		
Persons Served By One Dentist					
1976	2288	2724	3566	4057	4426
1981	2034	2257	2936	3325	3796

Source: Area Resource File, 1985.

politan counties in the state had six times the ratio of occupational therapists-to-population, four times the ratio of psychologists and speech pathologists, and greater than three times the ratio of opticians and physical therapists compared with nonmetropolitan areas.[10]

Viewed in totality, the health and medical care data that have been presented in Tables 3.3 and 3.4 and Figures 3.2 and 3.3 do not reflect favorably on the quality of life in the nonmetropolitan areas of the South. On virtually every measure examined here, both the rural LMAs and the black belt LMAs were shown to be ranked at the bottom. And projecting into the future, it is difficult to see how the existing gaps between the rural and urban South have much of a chance of disappearing.

WELFARE

The final set of data presented in this chapter deals very briefly with the need for, and provision of, welfare assistance in the various LMA groups. The purpose here is to identify and compare the extent to which the five different LMA groups are able to provide financial support to those in need. The rationale is that before the educational credentials and health status of a population can be improved, there must be adequate mechanisms to sustain existing levels of human capital in an area.

For illustrative purposes, two measures of need for welfare assistance are presented in Table 3.5. These are the percentage of the population living below the poverty line and the percentage of female headed households in the LMA group. The poverty measure is perhaps the most obvious indicant of need, since people who fall below the poverty line, by definition, lack sufficient income to maintain an adequate standard of living. Female-headed households was selected as an indicant of need because this group is considerably more likely to fall below the poverty line than male-headed households.

Not surprisingly, given the pattern of findings in Chapters 2 and 3, the black belt stands out as the LMA group with the greatest need of assistance for its residents. In 1980, the black belt LMAs had the highest percentage of female-headed households (14.5 percent) and a poverty rate (26.7 percent) that was nearly double that found in the large urban LMAs (Table 3.5). Because of their high degree of poverty, the rural LMAs also manifest a great deal of need. The urban LMAs,

Table 3.5
Social Welfare Indicators by LMA Group

	Urban			Rural	Black Belt
	Large	Mid-Size	Small		
Poverty Rate (1980)	13.7	14.4	17.4	18.9	26.7
% Female Headed Households (1980)	11.3	11.8	11.0	9.7	14.5
Average $ of Public Assistance (1980)	1905	1723	1694	1672	1574
% of Persons in Poverty Who Receive No Public Assistance	76.9	77.8	77.3	76.5	75.3

Source: U.S. Census of Population, 1980, PUMSD Computer Data File.

particularly the large urban LMAs, on the other hand, have considerably less poverty than the rural and black belt LMAs and comparatively fewer female-headed households compared with the black belt.

Despite the great need in the black belt and the rural LMAs, the average public assistance[11] is lowest in these areas. In 1980, average monthly aid to families with dependent children (AFDC) payments in the black belt were only $35. This was 31.4 percent less than the average AFDC payment in the large urban LMAs and 37 percent less than AFDC recipients in the mid-size urban LMAs receive.

Overall, average public assistance payments were lower in the black belt and rural areas than elsewhere. The $1,574/year received by the average black belt recipient is only 82.6 percent of the large urban average. Rural LMA residents who receive public assistance receive, on average, only 87.8 percent of the amount received in the large urban LMAs.

Finally, it is worth nothing that only about one-fourth of the persons in poverty received any public assistance in 1980. This percentage held across LMA groups. Because of the considerably higher level of poverty in the black belt and rural LMAs, this means that public assistance programs are doing relatively little to decrease the poverty gap between the large urban LMAs and the rural and black belt groups.

In short, the data in Table 3.5 show that the need for welfare assistance is greatest in the rural and black belt areas of the region. These are the places where poverty is highest and where groups of particularly disadvantaged people (i.e., female-headed households) are concentrated. Yet, despite this need, these areas have the lowest welfare benefits.

CONCLUSIONS

What the data in this chapter illustrate is that the economic development problems facing the rural and black belt LMAs in the South go beyond measures of economic well being such as income, poverty and unemployment. The rural and black belt areas are places where the populace is less educated than elsewhere in the region, where healthcare delivery and basic indicators of public health fall far short of urban standards, and where the welfare system fails to fully meet the needs of those who require assistance. Before these LMAs can expect to enter the social and economic mainstream of American society, these inadequacies will have to be confronted and rectified.

Addressing the deficiencies in human capital and welfare delivery in areas such as the rural South is admittedly a very difficult task. The last concerted effort to do so was President Lyndon Johnson's War on Poverty in the mid-1960s. At that time, federal programs such as food stamps and Head Start were instituted to begin to alleviate the chronic poverty that plagued the region and to begin to bolster the stock of human capital. The welfare system crafted and put into place during the Johnson years began unravelling shortly after Richard Nixon entered the White House and has continued to dissolve up to the present time. While some regions of the country have prospered in recent years, notably the Northeast and Southwest, the rural and black belt areas of the South have floundered and stagnated. The net result has been a widening gulf between the rural and urban South.

From a social justice viewpoint, it is undeniable that even the most marginal healthcare delivery systems, public education, and public welfare services offer help to those persons and groups at the bottom of the socioeconomic ladder. The question is not whether these efforts improve the life chances and standard of living of marginalized groups in the South. They clearly do. However, as the data presented in this chapter demonstrated, the access to health, education, and welfare systems and the levels of benefits derived from these systems varies across labor market groups.

Thus, even though children in the black belt and children in the large urban areas of the South have access to free public schooling through high school, the quality of that schooling and the level of local support for public education is generally superior in the urban centers. Likewise, healthcare manpower and facilities are available across the region. But the quality of healthcare and the access to specialized treatment facilities favors people living in urban locations over those residing in rural places.

It is a bit ironic that the provision of health, education, and welfare services lag in those places where they are most needed. Certainly, the black belt and rural LMAs require outside assistance if they hope to begin closing the gap in human resource development and general social welfare with the more urban places in the region. Given the recent trend toward further dismantling many federally sponsored programs and giving local communities more autonomy in meeting their own needs, it is unlikely that the less affluent and more rural places will be able to keep pace with the more prosperous and more urban areas. The gaps in human capital and general social welfare between the rural and black belt LMAs and the large and midsize urban places that seemed to close some during the federally sponsored War on Poverty, now seem likely to grow wider again.

The rural and black belt LMAs are caught in a bind. They have lured businesses to their areas through a set of de facto industrial policies. Part of the industrial policy agenda that was used to attract new employers was the promise of a low wage workforce and the granting of tax holidays. In the short term, this was a promising economic development strategy that created many nonagricultural employment opportunities. However, the types of employers that found the backwaters of the American South a good place to do business in the 1960s and 1970s have recently begun to bypass that region for Third World locations (where labor is even cheaper and the incentives even more lucrative than in the rural South). The rural and black belt labor markets are left with a reservoir of low-skilled workers for which there is little demand and a weak infrastructure (i.e., schools, healthcare facilities) that depends on large infusions of outside money to serve adequately the needs of the local population.

The standard of living and the stock of human capital in the rural and black belt South may never reach urban standards. The urban South will likely be able to offer amenities and a quality of life that surpasses the isolated areas of the region for some time to come. However, this does not mean that the rural and black belt areas cannot make significant strides toward improving the standards of living for their residents, and in so doing, begin to close the gap with the more urban places in the region. In any case, every effort must be made to ensure that the rural and black belt LMAs do not fall further behind.

NOTES

1. The President's National Advisory Commission on Rural Poverty, 1967, *The People Left Behind* (Washington, DC: U.S. Government Printing Office).
2. County and City Data Book.
3. For an overview of some of these issues, see J. Stephen Wright and Dale W. Lick, 1986, "Health in Rural America: Problems and Recommendations," in D.

Jahr, J. Johnson, and R. Wimberely (eds.), *New Dimensions in Rural Policy: Building Upon Our Heritage*, Joint Economic Committee of the U.S. Congress (Washington, DC: U.S. Government Printing Office), pp. 461-69.

4. The southern states are not bashful about using educational improvements as a business incentive. The state of Georgia recently ran a quarter-page advertisement in the *Wall Street Journal* (December 7, 1987, p. 20) under the banner "No State Has Ever Made A Smarter Investment." Part of the text of the ad noted that "new investments in education during our last four state budgets have totaled $1.6 billion without a tax increase." And, "In just four years, per pupil expenditures have risen 49%." Other impressive statistics were also presented. What the reader is not told is that Georgia still ranks 37th in per capita expenditures for education and pays its teachers 87 percent of the national average.

5. For a further elaboration on this point see, David L. Chiccoine and Gordon A. Hoke, 1986, "Rural Economies, Tax Structures, and Meeting the Demand for State-Local Government Services: A Focus on Local Schools," in Jahr, Johnson and Wimberely, (eds.), *New Dimensions in Rural Policy*, pp. 450-60.

6. See, for example, Robert Rosenthal and Lenore Jacobson, 1968, *Pygmalion in the Classroom: Teacher Expectation and Pupil's Intellectual Development* (New York: Holt, Rinehart and Winston).

7. The President's National Commission on Rural Poverty, p. 59.

8. Statement by Wendy Baldwin on "Trends and Correlates of Adolescent Pregnancy and Childbearing in the United States" before the House Subcommittee on Census and Population and the House Subcommittee on Health and the Environment, April 30, 1985.

9. For an overview of HMOs, see John B. McKinlay (ed.), *Health Maintenance Organizations* (Cambridge, MA: The MIT Press, 1981).

10. Cordes, S. M., and J. S. Wright, 1985, "Rural health concerns for the present and future," in J. Hamburg, D. J. Mase, and J. W. Perry (eds.), *Review of Allied Health Education* (Lexington, KY: University of Kentucky Press).

11. According to the U.S. Census Bureau, public assistance income includes cash receipts of payments made under the following public assistance programs: aid to families with dependent children (AFDC), old age assistance, general assistance, aid to the blind, and aid to the permanently and totally disabled. The payments are sometimes referred to as "supplementary security income" (SSI). They usually come from the federal government, but may also be received from state or local governments.

4. *Industrial Development and Occupational Change: Creating Job Opportunities for Southern Workers*

> For well over twenty years now the official policy of every state government in the South concerning industrialization has been to maximize the number of new firms that locate in the respective states. For the most part this policy has been administered without regard for the type of industry attracted to the region and without regard to the long range consequences of an industrial mix that might actually impede the socioeconomic development of the region rather than accelerate it.[1]

Prior to the 1960s, most rural areas of the South were generally devoid of industry. Nonagricultural employment opportunities in the region, especially those that paid above average wages, were concentrated in and around the major cities. In Georgia, for example, almost 40 percent of the state's durable manufacturing employment in 1960 was located in just five counties around Atlanta. Or, to put it differently, the remaining 60 percent of durable manufacturing employment was distributed among the other 154 counties in the state. In Alabama, almost 35 percent of durable manufacturing employment was located in just one county (Jefferson) in 1960. Beginning in the early 1960s, however, industrialization began to spread over the region. Not only did the cities and towns see their manufacturing base continue to expand, but the rural hinterlands also experienced tremendous growth. Between 1962 and 1978, for instance, almost one million new manufacturing jobs were created in rural areas of the South.[2]

While the various and sundry business incentives put into place by state and local governments during the 1950s and 1960s began to reap "rewards" in terms of non-farm job growth during the 1960s and 1970s, several impediments to industrial development had to be removed before the de facto industrial policies could work their magic. First, as I have noted in Chapter 2, cotton production shifted out of the region to Texas and the West. The diffusion of the mechanical cotton harvester and other technological advancements made it uneconomical to grow cotton in many areas of the region. This shift out of cotton was the prime catalyst behind the breakdown of the tenant/sharecropper system of agricultural production and it resulted in the creation of a pool of surplus labor in the region, albeit of a certain type—mainly uneducated and unskilled.

Second, during the 1960s, interstate highways began to crisscross the region. Isolated rural enclaves that were once inaccessible to all but the most determined industrialists, became tethered to the business and financial centers of the region by ribbons of asphalt and concrete. Today, the I-75, I-85, and I-95 corridors serve as vital economic arteries running through the rural South.

Finally, it was during the 1960s that racial segregation and the laws that supported it came under attack. Segregated school lunch counters and workplaces were a clear impediment to industrial development. As the racial barriers slowly came tumbling down in the 1960s and 1970s, however, race-conscious northern-based industries found it more acceptable to expand or relocate their operations in the South.

By virtually any standard of comparison, the scope and pace of industrial development in the South during the 1960s and 1970s was impressive. Not only did the manufacturing sector expand, but employment in many service industries surged. In the largest metropolitan counties of the region, for instance, over 75 percent of the new jobs created between 1970 and 1980 were in service industries. Even in the black belt, over half of the newly created jobs were service related.[3] Yet the benefits of an expanding economy were not evenly distributed across the region. Urban areas tended to attract the better paying jobs, those requiring well-educated and technologically sophisticated workers. Rural places, on the other hand, saw a proliferation of low-skill and low paying job opportunities.

One framework for understanding how and why economic development in the rural South was driven by goods production rather than services is the "filtering down" theory of industrial location that was introduced in Chapter 2. According to Wilbur Thompson, who was one of the first economists to describe the theory of industrial filtering:

> In national perspective, industries filter down through the system of cities, from places of greater to lesser industrial sophistication. Most often, the highest skills are needed in the difficult, early stage of mastering a new process, and skill requirements decline steadily as the production process is rationalized and routinized with experience. As the industry slides down the learning curve, the high wage rates of the more industrially sophisticated innovating areas become superfluous. The aging industry seeks out industrial backwaters where the cheaper labor is now up to the lesser demands of the simplified process.[4]

Based on the filtering down process of industrial development, it is difficult to see how rural and black belt LMAs could hope to match or even approach the occupational opportunity structure found in the large urban LMAs of the region. Further, it is an ironic commentary to note that industrial development policy as it has been formulated and implemented in the South has forced rural communities to compete against one another for a set of jobs that may do little to improve the lot of rural southern workers vis-à-vis their more urban counterparts.

The service sector of the economy, which now accounts for the bulk of jobs in all LMAs in the South and whose growth has outpaced manufacturing growth for several decades, offers little hope to rural and black belt workers. As I will illustrate in this chapter, most of the high wage, high-skill services tend to locate in and around the major metropolitan areas of the region. Financial, educational, legal, and other professional services have little reason to locate in the rural South.

A THUMBNAIL SKETCH OF THE INDUSTRIAL AND OCCUPATIONAL STRUCTURE IN THE SOUTH

The data in Table 4.1 provide a descriptive overview of the industrial and occupational structures in each of the five LMA types. As

Table 4.1
Occupational and Industrial Composition of Southern Labor Market Groups (1980)

Industry	Urban			Rural	Black Belt
	Large	Mid-Size	Small		
Agriculture	10.5%	8.7%	7.6%	6.9%	7.3%
Mining	.6	3.8	1.4	2.8	.7
Construction	7.3	7.4	7.5	7.5	7.0
Nondurable Manufacturing	7.2	13.0	13.0	15.4	13.4
Durable Manufacturing	9.0	9.7	10.4	13.0	10.7
Transportation	8.2	6.5	6.2	5.4	5.8
Wholesale Trade	4.9	4.1	3.4	3.0	4.2
Retail Trade	19.1	16.9	17.4	15.7	15.4
FIRE	6.8	5.4	4.2	3.0	3.8
Business Services	4.8	3.8	3.0	2.6	2.4
Personal Services	4.7	3.9	4.0	3.6	4.4
Entertainment	1.5	1.3	.9	.8	.5

Professional Services	18.5	19.0	18.5	17.5	19.2
Public Administration	4.9	5.5	5.5	3.8	5.2
Total	100.0	100.0	100.0	100.0	100.0
Occupation					
Manager	10.5%	8.7%	7.6%	6.9%	7.3%
Professional	10.9	10.8	9.8	8.7	9.2
Technical	2.8	2.8	2.5	2.0	2.1
Sales	12.3	10.4	9.9	8.6	9.4
Clerical	18.1	16.4	14.1	12.0	14.1
Service	14.9	14.0	14.7	13.6	13.9
Farmers	.4	1.1	1.7	2.7	3.0
Farm Workers	1.6	1.8	2.6	3.0	4.6
Craft	11.9	12.6	13.4	13.9	11.3
Operatives	16.6	21.4	23.7	28.6	25.1
Total	100.0	100.0	100.0	100.0	100.0

Source: U.S. Census of Population, 1980, PUMSD.

might be expected, industrial employment in the urban LMAs, particularly the large urban LMAs, is concentrated in the service sector of the economy. Nearly three out of every four workers in the large urban LMAs are employed in service related industries. In the rural and black belt LMAs, on the other hand, only around 60 percent of the labor force works in a service industry. And in several rural LMAs, more people work outside the service sector than in it.

Manufacturing industries are an important source of jobs for workers living outside the large urban LMAs. For instance, over 28 percent of the rural LMA workforce holds a manufacturing job. In contrast, in the largest urban LMAs in the South, only about 16 percent of the workforce is engaged in manufacturing pursuits.

Agriculture is also an important source of jobs in the rural and black belt LMAs. In the black belt, it ranks fifth (out of 14 industries) in the number of workers, while in the rural LMAs, it ranks sixth. On the other hand, in the large and mid-size urban LMAs, it ranks no higher than twelfth in the number of employees.

The occupational data in the bottom panel of Table 4.1 complement the industrial information. The urban LMAs, especially the large urban LMAs, have proportionately more white collar workers in general, and upper status professional, managerial, and technical workers in particular, than the rural and black belt LMAs. Professional, managerial, and technical positions account for almost one-fourth of the jobs in the large urban LMAs. In the rural and black belt LMAs, these positions constitute 17.6 and 18.6 percent of the workforce, respectively.

At the other end of the occupational spectrum are the low wage, low-skill blue collar jobs. About 30 percent of the rural and black belt workers are engaged in these types of unskilled or semi-skilled activities, either as factory laborers or as farmworkers. In the large urban LMAs, however, only 17 percent of the workers hold these types of jobs.

In short, this thumbnail sketch of the industrial and occupational structure in the South reveals considerable variations across LMA types. These findings are consistent with the filtering down theory of industrial location, and they suggest important differences across LMAs in the nature and range of employment opportunities confronting southern workers. In the next sections of this chapter I will probe more carefully into recent changes in these employment opportunities.

MANUFACTURING EMPLOYMENT

Despite the fact that manufacturing employment across the South is slipping relative to employment in other industries, it should be noted that between 1975 and 1984 over 600,000 new manufacturing jobs were created in the region. Even in the large urban LMAs, where the percentage of manufacturing workers is lowest, nearly 100,000 manufacturing positions were added to the economy during this period. However, as the data in Tables 4.2 and 4.3 show, the types of employment opportunities in the manufacturing sector varied considerably by LMA group.

Manufacturing employment across the large urban LMAs in the South is concentrated in both durable and nondurable industries. Transportation equipment and electrical equipment industries were the largest manufacturing employers in 1984, accounting for over one-fourth of all manufacturing employment. Interestingly, the data in Table 4.3 show that between 1975 and 1984 employment levels in these two durable manufacturing industries expanded by over 60,000 jobs and accounted for over 65 percent of all manufacturing growth in the large urban LMAs. It is worth noting that the average wages in the electrical and transportation equipment industries are not only among the highest in the region, but are well above the average manufacturing wages in the large urban LMAs.

At the other end of the manufacturing spectrum, two nondurable industries, food and textiles, lost about 18,000 workers in the large urban LMAs between 1975 and 1984. In fact, textiles have declined to the point where they now account for less than two percent of total manufacturing in the large urban LMAs. Wages in the food and textile industries were well below the average manufacturing wages in this LMA group. This finding suggests that at least part of the exacerbation of income differences between the large urban LMAs and the rural and black belt LMAs noted in Chapter 2 can be attributed to the ability of large urban areas to shed low wage industries and replace them with higher paying firms.

In the mid-size and small urban LMAs, the food, chemical, textile, and apparel industries were the largest employers in the mid-1980s. Employment in the textile industry had declined by 30,000 workers in these LMAs, however, between 1975 and 1984, while the apparel industry added almost 38,000 workers during this same period. This is a case of low-wage textile jobs being replaced by even lower-wage

Table 4.2
Percentage Distribution and Average Earnings of Selected Manufacturing Industries by Labor Market Area

Manufacturing Industry		Urban			Rural	Black Belt
		Large	Mid-Size	Small		
Food	%	9.8	7.6	8.2	9.1	10.8
	$	10,861	9,288	8,384	7,732	7,215
Textiles	%	1.4	12.4	9.2	10.5	11.7
	$	7,573	8,412	8,579	8,244	8,702
Transportation Equipment	%	12.1	7.1	7.6	3.5	2.8
	$	14,184	12,757	11,659	10,235	11,754
Electrical Equipment	%	13.3	7.5	7.7	7.8	4.7
	$	13,200	11,291	11,296	9,024	10,002
Machinery	%	7.6	7.8	5.9	6.2	6.1
	$	13,481	12,701	11,624	10,352	10,014
Fabricated Metals	%	7.3	5.3	5.8	4.6	5.7
	$	11,975	11,323	10,944	9,842	8,026

Printing	%	8.9	5.9	4.8	3.9	2.3
	$	10,001	9,871	7,972	8,428	5,960
Apparel	%	6.4	7.8	12.2	16.8	18.2
	$	6,700	5,852	5,191	5,110	5,722
Chemicals	%	5.5	9.4	7.2	4.1	4.8
	$	13,983	16,092	15,079	12,648	11,526
Lumber	%	3.7	4.7	7.4	8.8	13.2
	$	10,719	8,062	8,402	8,070	7,399
Furniture	%	3.3	3.3	2.8	5.5	2.8
	$	8,654	8,096	7,145	7,873	8,376
All Other	%	20.7	21.2	21.2	19.2	16.9
Total	%	100.0	100.0	100.0	100.0	100.0
Average Mfg. Earnings	$	11,483	10,354	9,806	8,450	8,515

Sources: County Business Patterns, 1984; U.S. Census of Population, 1980, PUMSD.

Table 4.3
Employment Changes in Selected Manufacturing Industries Between 1975 and 1984 by Labor Market Area

Manufacturing Industries		Urban			Rural	Black Belt	Total
		Large	Mid-Size	Small			
Food	(N)	-6,482	6,824	8,178	14,708	4,429	27,657
	(Δ%)	-6.7	4.1	4.1	9.5	22.7	
Textiles	(N)	-11,481	-19,835	-10,874	2,724	-1,578	-41,044
	(Δ%)	-11.9	-11.8	-5.5	1.8	-8.1	
Transportation Equipment	(N)	20,767	29,813	44,652	8,973	-511	103,693
	(Δ%)	21.6	18.2	22.5	5.8	-2.6	
Electrical Equipment	(N)	41,303	27,011	38,668	17,219	3,001	127,202
	(Δ%)	42.9	16.4	19.5	11.1	15.4	
Machinery	(N)	4,128	25,131	17,414	12,215	1,580	60,468
	(Δ%)	4.3	15.3	8.8	7.9	8.1	

Fabricated Metals	(N) (Δ%)	1,361 1.4	13,809 8.4	12,031 6.1	6,858 4.4	3,192 16.4	37,251
Printing	(N) (Δ%)	26,269 27.3	14,591 8.9	18,891 9.5	11,418 7.4	611 3.1	71,780
Apparel	(N) (Δ%)	4,194 4.3	14,514 8.8	23,330 11.7	23,111 14.9	5,456 28.1	70,605
Chemicals	(N) (Δ%)	2,263 2.3	8,576 5.2	1,928 1.0	7,580 4.9	-533 -2.7	19,814
Lumber	(N) (Δ%)	7,004 7.3	8,678 5.3	17,723 8.9	11,286 7.3	2,335 12.0	47,016
Furniture	(N) (Δ%)	6,958 7.2	10,986 6.7	5,061 2.6	14,693 9.4	-1,419 -7.3	35,979
All Manu- facturing	(N) (Δ%)	96,354 15.2	164,128 25.9	198,178 31.3	154,780 24.4	19,426 3.1	632,866

Source: County Business Patterns, 1975 and 1984.

apparel jobs. Although the food and chemical industries are important employers who pay average or above average wages in the mid-size and small urban LMAs, they experienced only modest growth between 1975 and 1984. The greatest expansion in employment took place in the electrical and transportation equipment industries. This was good news for workers in these labor market areas since these industries pay above average wages.

In the rural and black belt LMAs, manufacturing employment is concentrated in the nondurable industries, especially in the apparel, textile, lumber, and food sectors. Not only are these industries at the low end of the wage spectrum, but with the exception of the textile industry, all registered sizable employment increases between 1975 and 1984. In fact, the low wage apparel industry, which already is the largest employer in virtually all rural and black belt LMAs, added more jobs in these LMAs than any other manufacturing industry between 1975 and 1984. The apparel industry accounted for nearly 15 percent of all new manufacturing jobs created in the rural LMAs during this period and for almost 30 percent of the new manufacturing jobs in the black belt. This is one more case where an already sizable disparity in the nature and range of industrial employment opportunities between the rural and urban South appears to be growing larger.

SERVICE EMPLOYMENT

The largest employment gains across LMA groups in the South were registered in the service sector (Tables 4.4 and 4.5). In the large urban LMAs, for example, there were ten new service jobs created for every manufacturing job between 1975 and 1984. In the mid-size and small urban LMAs the ratio of new service jobs to new manufacturing jobs was roughly five to one. In the black belt the ratio was three to one. Even in the rural LMAs there were two new service jobs created for every new manufacturing job between 1975 and 1984.

The distribution of service industries varies across LMA groups. Wage levels within these industries also varies by LMA group. Retail trade, for example, constitutes a larger part of the service economy in the rural, black belt, and small urban LMAs than in the mid-size and large urban LMAs. And average wage levels in the retail trade industry, although relatively low vis-à-vis wages in most other service industries, are higher in the large and mid-size urban LMAs than in the rural and black belt LMAs. The average retail worker in the rural LMAs, for example, earns just 80 percent of what a retail worker in the large urban LMA earns, while the typical black belt retail worker earns only 86 percent as much.

While retail trade is proportionately more important in the rural and black belt LMAs, business and repair services are more important to the large and mid-size urban LMAs. On average, about one in 10 service workers in the large urban LMAs is affiliated with some sort of business service. Among the rural LMAs, on the other hand, less than one in 20 service workers is employed in the business and repair service sector. Furthermore, it should be noted that average earnings in business and repair service industries exceed average service sector wages in all of the LMA groups (Table 4.4).

Along with the retail trade industry, the hospitality industry, which includes eating and drinking establishments and hotels and motels, is an important source of service employment in all LMA groups in the region. It is also the service industry with very low wages, though the wage figures in Table 4.3 may understate somewhat the true wage levels since they do not include money earned as gratuities. In any case, it is worth noting that reported wages are highest in the large urban LMAs and lowest in the rural and black belt LMAs. The typical worker in a rural LMA earns only 68 percent of what a hospitality worker in the large urban LMAs earns (Table 4.4). Further, it should be noted that the relative increase in hospitality employment has been greatest outside of the large urban LMAs (Table 4.5). Again, as was the case of low wage manufacturing employment, it appears that the rural and black belt LMAs are succeeding in attracting service jobs, but these jobs exacerbate rather than ameliorate the overall wage differentials among the LMA groups.

The largest service industry across all LMA groups is professional services. This is a broad category of economic activity that includes healthcare, education, and legal services, among others. This branch of the service economy represents about 22 percent of all service employment across the South. Furthermore, about three in ten new service jobs in all of the LMA groups were affiliated with this sector. While this powerful engine of service sector growth seems equitably distributed across labor market areas, the earning potential of these jobs varies from one LMA group to another. The highest wages are found in the urban LMAs, particularly the large urban LMAs, while

Table 4.4
Percentage Distribution and Average Earnings of Service Industries by Labor Market Area

Service Industry		Urban			Rural	Black Belt
		Large	Mid-Size	Small		
Transportation	%	11.2	9.5	9.2	8.9	9.5
	$	14,784	13,703	12,929	12,419	11,758
Wholesale Trade	%	11.0	10.5	9.3	10.0	11.5
	$	12,919	12,280	10,542	10,007	10,258
Retail Trade	%	19.4	22.1	27.1	28.6	28.8
	$	7,945	7,258	6,762	6,356	6,884
Hospitality	%	12.9	12.5	13.3	13.3	10.5
	$	4,910	3,949	3,748	3,318	3,434
Recreation	%	1.8	1.8	1.4	1.7	1.5
	$	6,476	6,023	4,628	5,035	4,666

Personal	%	2.1	2.3	2.3	2.2	2.3
	$	4,812	4,414	3,830	3,815	2,971
Professional	%	21.2	22.0	21.6	21.9	22.3
Services	$	10,062	9,138	8,344	7,872	7,579
Business and	%	9.8	9.0	6.3	4.7	4.7
Repair Services	$	9,903	9,354	8,174	7,772	8,672
Finance, Insurance	%	10.6	10.3	9.5	8.7	8.9
and Real Estate	$	11,657	11,196	12,195	9,455	11,528
Total	%	100.0	100.0	100.0	100.0	100.0
Average Service Earnings	$	9,723	8,876	8,003	7,509	7,742

Sources: County Business Patterns, 1984; U.S. Census of Population 1980, PUMSD.

Table 4.5
Employment Changes in Service Industries Between 1975 and 1984 by Labor Market Area

Service Industry		Urban			Rural	Black Belt
		Large	Mid-Size	Small		
Transportation	N	75,413	45,513	51,406	28,023	4,805
	(Δ%)	7.2	5.6	5.7	8.8	8.4
Wholesale Trade	N	89,500	53,388	50,621	20,667	2,569
	(Δ%)	8.5	6.6	5.6	6.5	4.5
Retail Trade	N	148,285	117,514	169,085	68,044	10,727
	(Δ%)	14.1	14.5	18.7	21.4	18.6
Hospitality	N	166,693	151,926	168,270	62,782	9,604
	(Δ%)	15.9	18.7	18.5	19.7	16.7

Recreation	N (Δ%)	15,646 1.5	9,968 1.2	12,238 1.4	4,259 1.3	988 1.7
Personal Services	N (Δ%)	13,273 1.3	7,889 1.0	8,614 .9	2,076 .6	28 .05
Professional Services	N (Δ%)	292,785 28.0	241,314 29.7	273,933 30.2	92,774 29.1	16,221 28.1
Business and Repair Services	N (Δ%)	147,226 14.1	121,918 15.0	96,716 10.7	21,019 6.6	7,402 12.8
Finance, Insurance and Real Estate	N (Δ%)	99,761 9.5	61,937 7.6	74,746 8.2	18,732 5.9	5,198 9.0
All Services	N (Δ%)	1,048,582 47.1	811,367 45.0	905,629 46.8	318,376 46.2	57,542 26.0

Source: County Business Patterns, 1975 and 1984.

the rural and black belt LMAs offer lower wage professional service job opportunities. A professional service worker in the black belt, for instance, earns only about 75 percent of what his/her counterpart in the large urban LMAs earns. Over time, such a relative disparity in wage levels will lead to an even greater absolute gap in earnings between workers in the rural and urban South.

HIGH TECHNOLOGY EMPLOYMENT

In recent years, policymakers and industrial recruiters throughout the country have turned their attention to high technology enterprises as a panacea to economic development problems. Michael Dukakis, in his bid for the presidency in 1988, frequently pointed with pride to how the high technology sector had transformed his state's economy. The economic boom that accompanied the influx of high technology companies into the Silicon Valley is legendary among economic development officials. In the South, the Research Triangle area in North Carolina, central Florida, and Huntsville, Alabama, have emerged as "high-tech" hubs.

The term "high technology" is a nebulous one and has been used to refer to a broad range of manufacturing and service enterprises. These enterprises are generally at the "cutting edge" of the economy in terms of innovation and technology. The Bureau of Labor Statistics has identified three characteristics that are commonly associated with high technology industries: 1) a larger proportion of scientific, engineering, and technical workers than other industries; 2) a high level of research and development expenditures; and 3) a highly sophisticated product.[5] As Len Bloomquist, a research sociologist for the Economic Research Service of the U.S. Department of Agriculture, notes, "These criteria suggest that high technology industries are distinguished from most other industries by their occupational structures and emphasis on product development and innovations."[6] Placed within the "filtering down" theory of industrial location, one would expect that high technology firms would find it most advantageous to locate in major metropolitan areas where skilled labor is most plentiful.

In an attempt to better understand how employment opportunities in high technology industries are distributed across LMAs in the South, I have divided a set of industries commonly considered to form the core of the "high technology" sector, into three segments:

1) manufacturing; 2) communications; and 3) services.[7] The results presented in Table 4.6 reaffirm what others have noted, namely that high-tech employment opportunities are concentrated in and around the large urban places in the region.[8] In the large urban LMAs, total high technology employment grew by 51.2 percent between 1975 and 1984. This is more than double the rate of high-tech growth in the rural LMAs and it is three times the growth rate for black belt LMAs. Looked at a bit differently, in 1975 the large urban LMAs contained 24.8 percent of all high-tech jobs in the region. By 1984 they accounted for 28 percent. Most of the high technology growth in the South took place in the manufacturing sector, although high technology services also registered significant increases. Again, it was in the urban LMAs, particularly the large urban LMAs, where much of this growth took place.

In the large urban LMAs, high technology manufacturing accounted for about half of all high-tech jobs in the mid-1980s, while the service segment accounted for slightly over 20 percent. In the small and mid-size urban LMAs, manufacturing employment was about 60 percent of all high-tech employment, while service jobs represented between 11.6 and 17.8 percent of high technology employment. In the rural LMAs, two out of every three high technology jobs were in manufacturing, while one in twelve was service related. In the black belt, high technology manufacturing accounted for nearly 60 percent of all employment, while high technology services accounted for less than 10 percent.

It is worth noting that the slowest growing segment of the high technology sector across all LMA groups in the South was communications. This slow growth is probably due in large measure to extensive automation within the telecommunications industry. Nevertheless, it should be remembered that in 1984 over 350,000 southern workers were employed in this segment. And in the black belt, communications employment is a vital part of the high technology sector, accounting for one in three high technology jobs.

RACE AND SEX SEGMENTATION
IN THE OCCUPATIONAL STRUCTURE

A long-standing feature of the U.S. occupational structure has been the pervasiveness of race and sex segregation in the labor force.[9]

Table 4.6
Distribution of High Technology Employment Across LMA Groups in the South

High Technology Employment		Urban			Rural	Black Belt
		Large	Mid-Size	Small		
Total	1984	337,002	1,106,384	360,996	147,130	29,033
	1975	222,900	258,683	272,457	117,965	25,405
	Δ(N)	114,102	72,423	88,539	29,165	3,628
	Δ(%)	51.2	28.0	32.4	24.7	14.3
Manufacturing	1984	179,957	204,402	249,606	110,346	18,669
	1975	105,974	159,634	184,613	86,256	15,825
	Δ(N)	73,983	44,768	64,993	24,090	2,844
	Δ(%)	69.8	28.0	35.2	27.9	18.0
Communications	1984	89,164	71,426	75,582	27,760	7,323
	1975	86,423	70,377	69,683	26,060	6,873
	Δ(N)	2,741	869	5,899	1,700	450
	Δ(%)	3.2	1.2	8.5	6.5	6.5
Services	1984	67,881	55,458	35,808	9,024	3,041
	1975	30,503	28,672	18,161	5,649	2,707
	Δ(N)	37,378	26,786	17,647	3,375	334
	Δ(%)	122.5	93.4	97.2	59.7	12.3

Source: County Business Patterns, 1975 and 1984.

Creating Jobs 93

This segmentation is particularly germane to issues of economic development and social justice in the South, since industries that locate in rural and black belt areas of the region tend to employ large numbers of blacks and women in low wage and low-skill jobs.

The data in Table 4.7 show the percentages of different race/sex groups in various occupations and the average yearly wages these workers receive. Several generalizations are readily apparent. First, white men are overrepresented in the best occupational positions (e.g., upper white collar and skilled blue collar positions), regardless of LMA group. Second, white men earn more across all occupational categories than the other race/sex groups. The earnings differential is particularly large in professional, managerial, and technical jobs. Third, the modal occupational category for white women across all LMA groups is sales/clerical. For black women, the modal category is service worker, while for black men it is operatives. Finally, earnings for blacks and white women are roughly equivalent within each occupational category across LMA groups. However, because black women are concentrated in lower-wage service worker jobs, their overall average earnings are considerably below the other race/sex groups.

Although there are similarities in the way race and sex are related to occupational allocation and earnings across LMA groups, there are noteworthy differences among the LMA groups as well. For instance, within racial categories, the percentage of women in professional, managerial, and technical jobs, service worker jobs, skilled blue collar jobs, or agricultural jobs is fairly similar across LMA groups. However, the proportion of black and white women in sales/clerical occupations and operative jobs varies from one LMA group to another, and especially between the large urban LMAs and the rural LMAs. In the large urban LMAs a large proportion of white and black women are employed as sales or clerical workers, while comparatively few hold operative jobs. In the rural LMAs, on the other hand, a substantial proportion of women workers hold operative jobs. Looked at in a bit more detail, nearly 50 percent of all white women in the large urban LMAs are in the sales/clerical category while only nine percent are classified as operatives. In the rural LMAs, only 33.7 percent of the white women hold sales or clerical jobs while nearly 25 percent work as operatives. What this means is that when lower level white collar jobs are available, women, especially white women, are the preferred incumbents. When these types of jobs are not available, women are allocated to operative positions. Interestingly, female earnings for

Table 4.7
Occupational Distribution and Average Earnings Per Occupation by Race, Sex, and LMA Group

Occupational Group	White Male %	White Male $	White Female %	White Female $	Black Male %	Black Male $	Black Female %	Black Female $
			Large Urban LMA					
Prof/Tech/Man	28.1	21,207	24.2	8,977	10.6	13,471	18.0	9,311
Sales/Clerical	19.7	14,703	48.2	6,088	12.2	9,407	29.1	5,996
Service Worker	9.5	7,864	15.4	3,961	17.9	6,019	35.5	3,784
Craftsworker	21.4	13,868	2.2	6,687	14.9	10,258	2.0	7,316
Operative	18.8	10,381	9.0	5,184	39.9	8,733	14.2	5,263
Agricultural Worker	2.5	7,905	1.0	4,255	4.5	4,200	1.2	2,845
			Mid-Size Urban LMA					
Prof/Tech/Man	25.6	19,996	23.6	8,567	9.6	12,683	15.2	8,677
Sales/Clerical	17.1	14,353	43.4	5,801	9.9	9,687	23.9	5,761
Service Worker	8.0	7,342	14.4	3,356	17.6	5,287	34.0	3,413
Craftsworker	23.0	13,090	2.5	6,946	16.4	9,036	2.8	6,022
Operative	22.3	9,759	15.0	5,513	41.2	7,722	22.3	5,456
Agricultural Worker	4.0	7,398	1.1	2,774	5.3	3,760	1.8	1,597

	Small Urban LMA					
Prof/Tech/Man	21.8	18,748	21.8	7,781	7.6	11,227	14.8	8,197
Sales/Clerical	14.6	13,218	41.2	5,208	6.7	8,317	17.4	4,772
Service Worker	7.8	7,284	16.7	3,193	16.4	4,999	37.7	3,224
Craftsworker	24.3	12,539	2.4	6,172	15.8	8,780	2.5	6,068
Operative	25.3	10,072	16.5	5,062	43.9	7,481	24.7	5,150
Agricultural Worker	6.2	8,462	1.3	3,305	9.6	4,163	2.9	1,693
	Rural LMA					
Prof/Tech/Man	17.8	17,407	19.5	7,508	6.7	10,145	10.8	7,384
Sales/Clerical	12.1	11,821	33.7	4,689	5.3	6,875	13.4	3,947
Service Worker	7.6	6,490	17.7	2,813	16.1	4,739	35.9	3,061
Craftsworker	24.3	11,528	2.8	6,545	14.4	8,170	3.0	4,897
Operative	29.9	9,353	24.1	4,965	46.0	7,124	32.9	4,974
Agricultural Worker	8.3	7,188	2.2	3,653	11.5	3,591	4.0	1,406
	Black Belt LMA					
Prof/Tech/Man	23.4	18,138	22.9	8,139	8.7	10,443	15.0	3,842
Sales/Clerical	18.0	13,942	47.1	5,550	6.1	7,911	16.3	4,720
Service Worker	5.9	7,999	11.4	3,271	11.1	4,725	33.5	2,805
Craftsworker	21.8	12,687	2.1	5,591	15.0	7,431	3.2	4,023
Operative	21.2	9,885	14.7	4,998	43.4	6,182	27.3	5,093
Agricultural Worker	9.7	10,808	1.8	3,624	15.7	3,789	4.7	1,408

Source: U.S. Census of Population, 1980, PUMSD.

sales/clerical jobs are higher than for operative jobs in the urban LMAs, while female operatives earn more in rural LMAs than sales/clerical workers.

One further point is worth noting in Table 4.7. In the black belt LMAs, nearly 60 percent of black men are employed in agricultural or operative occupations. Average wages for black male operatives in the black belt are 71 percent of the wages black male operatives receive in the large urban LMAs and they are 62 percent of the earnings of white male operatives in the black belt. To be black and male and to live in the black belt is to be confronted with an extremely limited range of low wage employment alternatives.

OCCUPATIONAL SEGREGATION IN THE MANUFACTURING SECTOR

Having examined how men and women and blacks and whites are distributed across occupational groupings in the five sets of LMAs, it is useful to look at patterns of race and sex segregation within specific industrial sectors. The data in Table 4.8 are the occupational distributions for manufacturing industries. The most striking feature here is the extremely large concentration of blacks in the operative category. Most operatives are semi-skilled or unskilled blue collar factory workers. In fact, black women appear to have few other occupational alternatives in manufacturing industries other than as operatives, regardless of the LMA they work in.

Not unexpectedly, white men are disproportionately found in the best white collar jobs in the manufacturing sector and most of the highly skilled blue collar positions as well. Even in the black belt, where black labor is abundant, white men in professional, managerial, and technical positions outnumber black men by almost five to one. And there are over twice as many white men in skilled blue collar slots as there are black men.

The percentage of female operatives, both black and white, is higher in the rural LMAs than in the other LMA groups. This finding is consistent with the filtering down/product cycle theory of industrial location and suggests that low wage, semi-skilled, female workers are the preferred labor supply for the peripheral manufacturing enterprises that set up shop in the rural South.

Lastly, it should be noted that white women, much more than black women, are the favored incumbents for sales and clerical positions within the manufacturing sector. This holds true across all LMA groups, and especially in the black belt LMAs. Clearly, black women are relegated to the least desirable jobs in manufacturing across the South, and black women in the black belt have virtually no occupational alternatives open to them other than as low-skill, low wage, blue collar workers.

OCCUPATIONAL SEGREGATION IN THE SERVICE SECTOR

Within the service industries, occupational segregation along race and sex lines is not as dramatic as it is in manufacturing (Table 4.9). Nevertheless, there are distinct patterns in the ways men and women and blacks and whites are distributed across the occupational structure in the service sector. For white men, in all LMA groups, the modal occupational category is professional, managerial, and technical work. Furthermore, whites in general, and white men in particular, are more likely to occupy these upper level white collar positions than blacks. For white women the modal occupational category is sales and clerical, while for black women it is service worker. Black men are concentrated in the service worker and operative categories.

On the surface, it appears that there is only minor variation across LMA groups in race and sex occupational distributions in the service industries. However, it is worth noting that blacks are underrepresented in the service sector of the black belt, while their representation in the other LMA groups approximates their overall proportion in the labor force. For example, 40 percent of the black belt labor force is black, yet only 35 percent of the workers in service industries in the black belt are black. In the large urban LMAs, on the other hand, 18 percent of the labor force is black and 18 percent of all service industry workers are black. Thus, it appears that occupational opportunities for blacks living in the black belt in the fast growing service sector of the economy may be more restricted than elsewhere in the South. This is unfortunate since service industries tend to have a more favorable occupational structure for blacks than manufacturing industries.

Table 4.8
Occupational Distribution in Manufacturing Industries by Race, Sex, and LMA Group

Occupational Group	Large Urban LMA			
	White Male %	White Female %	Black Male %	Black Female %
Prof/Tech/Man	23.6	9.7	4.2	2.9
Sales/Clerical	12.9	31.8	7.4	14.5
Service Worker	2.9	1.0	4.1	2.3
Craftsworker	24.8	7.0	14.7	7.3
Operative	35.4	50.4	69.2	72.9
Agricultural Worker	.4	.1	.4	.1
	Mid-Size Urban LMA			
Prof/Tech/Man	19.1	7.5	3.6	2.7
Sales/Clerical	10.5	22.5	5.6	7.8
Service Worker	3.2	.8	6.4	3.8
Craftsworker	27.2	7.1	16.0	6.7
Operative	39.4	62.1	66.6	78.8
Agricultural Worker	.6	--	1.8	.2

	Small Urban LMA			
Prof/Tech/Man	16.5	5.3	2.6	1.8
Sales/Clerical	7.7	20.2	3.7	5.3
Service Worker	3.5	1.2	5.6	3.3
Craftsworker	27.1	6.1	16.6	7.1
Operative	43.8	67.2	68.1	82.2
Agricultural Worker	1.4	.06	3.4	.3

	Rural LMA			
Prof/Tech/Man	12.1	3.6	2.7	.7
Sales/Clerical	6.9	14.2	5.9	4.0
Service Worker	4.1	.8	6.7	3.2
Craftsworker	23.2	6.7	12.0	5.9
Operative	51.3	74.6	69.0	85.9
Agricultural Worker	2.4	.1	3.7	.3

	Black Belt LMA			
Prof/Tech/Man	15.2	1.1	3.3	1.0
Sales/Clerical	11.6	23.2	6.0	3.8
Service Worker	4.6	.4	3.5	2.2
Craftsworker	26.4	5.7	12.6	7.9
Operative	39.8	65.2	70.6	84.7
Agricultural Worker	2.4	.4	4.0	.4

Source: U.S. Census of Population, 1980, PUMSD.

Table 4.9
Occupational Distribution in Service Industries by Race, Sex, and LMA Group

Occupational Group	Large Urban LMA			
	White Male %	White Female %	Black Male %	Black Female %
Prof/Tech/Man	33.5	26.8	14.9	20.5
Sales/Clerical	25.8	50.7	16.8	31.6
Service Worker	13.5	18.0	26.9	41.2
Craftsworker	12.8	1.4	9.5	1.1
Operative	13.8	3.0	30.4	5.4
Agricultural Worker	.6	.1	1.5	.2
	Mid-Size Urban LMA			
Prof/Tech/Man	33.3	28.2	15.4	19.2
Sales/Clerical	24.2	48.7	15.4	28.9
Service Worker	12.2	18.3	29.5	43.6
Craftsworker	14.2	1.2	10.8	1.5
Operative	15.4	3.5	27.7	6.7
Agricultural Worker	.7	.1	1.2	.1

	Small Urban LMA			
Prof/Tech/Man	29.9	26.7	13.4	19.7
Sales/Clerical	23.2	46.9	11.3	22.0
Service Worker	12.4	21.4	30.4	50.8
Craftsworker	15.4	1.3	10.0	.9
Operative	18.4	3.6	33.0	6.4
Agricultural Worker	.7	.1	1.9	.2
	Rural LMA			
Prof/Tech/Man	28.3	26.8	13.4	17.1
Sales/Clerical	21.5	42.4	7.3	19.3
Service Worker	13.1	25.7	33.2	56.2
Craftsworker	15.3	1.0	9.2	1.3
Operative	21.0	4.0	33.7	6.0
Agricultural Worker	.8	.1	3.2	.1
	Black Belt LMA			
Prof/Tech/Man	32.3	27.9	18.2	21.8
Sales/Clerical	27.1	53.6	10.2	22.1
Service Worker	8.3	14.6	23.9	48.2
Craftsworker	15.2	.9	11.3	1.2
Operative	16.4	3.0	34.3	6.4
Agricultural Worker	.7	--	2.1	.3

Source: U.S. Census of Population, 1980, PUMSD.

OCCUPATIONAL SEGREGATION IN THE HIGH-TECHNOLOGY SECTOR

If there is one set of industries in which one would expect blacks and women to fare better than elsewhere in the economy, it is in the high-tech sector. High-tech enterprises are defined, in part, by their highly skilled, technologically sophisticated, and well-educated labor force. Hence, they should have occupational structures in which professional, technical, and skilled blue collar jobs predominate.

It is clear from the data in Table 4.10 that high technology means different things in different LMA groups. In the large and mid-size urban LMAs, high technology employment is concentrated in professional, technical, managerial, and skilled blue collar positions. For example, nearly 70 percent of the white men and about 40 percent of the black men in these urban LMAs occupy these highly skilled jobs. This is the widely held view of high-tech employment. Outside of these two LMA groups and especially in the rural LMAs, however, the occupational profile of the high technology industries changes dramatically.

In the rural LMAs, for example, the modal occupational category for black and white women and for black men is operative. Furthermore, in the rural LMAs more white men are employed as operatives than as managers, professionals, or technicians combined. From these findings it seems that when high-tech industries locate in rural areas of the South they bring along only their high-tech designation and leave their set of high-tech occupational opportunities behind in the cities. Furthermore, it is worth noting that in many ways the high-tech occupational profile in the rural South is similar in many respects to the occupational profile for manufacturing industries in general (see Table 4.8).

Interestingly, the occupational profile for high-tech industries in the black belt compares favorably with the high-tech occupational profile in the urban LMA groups. This is a bit surprising, given the findings for the rural LMAs. However, two factors may account for this seeming aberration. First, high-tech industries, in general, have not located in the black belt. In fact, only 2.4 percent of all high-tech employment in the South is found in the black belt. Second, the communications segment represents a larger share of total high tech employment in the black belt than elsewhere (Table 4.6). The general dearth of high technology employment opportunities coupled with a high-tech industrial mix in which communications plays a significant part has produced what on the surface appears to be a situation in which blacks stand to benefit. To put it in another perspective, however, it should be noted that only one in 35 blacks in the black belt holds any type of high technology job and the majority who do work in the high technology sector hold relatively low skilled jobs.

FARMING AND AGRIBUSINESS: WHITHER THE FUTURE OF AGRICULTURE IN THE SOUTH

Although the number of farmers and farmworkers declined precipitously across the South during the 1950s and 1960s, as cotton production left the region, agricultural employment began to stabilize a bit during the 1970s. In fact, some segments of the farm sector actually saw employment increase during this period. The number of part-time farmers, for example, increased by over 125,000 between 1970 and 1980.[10] Overall, however, the number of full-time farmers has continued to dwindle across the region during the 1980s. Despite the decline in farm numbers, it should be noted that in many rural areas of the South, and especially in the black belt, agriculture remains the most important part of the local economic base. Furthermore, a large percentage of the local labor force in this area is employed directly in production agriculture, while another large segment is employed in the agribusiness sector.

Today, the structure of agricultural production in the South is best described as "bimodal." According to John Lee, head of the Economic Research Service of the U.S. Department of Agriculture:

> The distribution of farms by sales class is becoming increasingly bimodal. A few large producers provide most of the commercial farm output. A large number of small producers account for little product in the aggregate and their economic well-being is only tangentially related to agriculture and traditional farm programs.[11]

In the vernacular of researchers and policymakers, the term "dual structure of agriculture" has come to characterize the current farm situation in the United States.[12] On one side of the dual structure of agriculture are the part-time, limited resource, "hobby" farmers. On

Table 4.10
Occupational Distribution in High Technology Industries by Race, Sex, and LMA Group

Occupational Group	Large Urban LMA			
	White Male %	White Female %	Black Male %	Black Female %
Prof/Tech/Man	46.4	17.6	20.2	10.5
Sales/Clerical	14.1	53.9	8.9	44.4
Service Worker	1.9	.5	5.2	1.7
Craftsworker	23.0	6.3	24.4	5.6
Operative	14.6	21.7	41.3	37.8
	Mid-Size Urban LMA			
Prof/Tech/Man	41.4	17.2	17.6	9.4
Sales/Clerical	11.5	44.6	11.5	37.4
Service Worker	2.1	.5	7.6	2.3
Craftsworker	27.1	7.2	22.3	8.4
Operative	17.9	30.5	41.0	42.5

	Small Urban LMA		
Prof/Tech/Man	35.9	13.5	13.6	8.9
Sales/Clerical	11.0	39.4	7.3	26.3
Service Worker	2.6	1.1	6.0	4.4
Craftsworker	26.7	6.8	22.8	7.0
Operative	23.8	39.2	50.1	53.4

	Rural LMA		
Prof/Tech/Man	28.4	8.0	10.0	2.4
Sales/Clerical	8.7	29.2	9.0	8.0
Service Worker	3.3	.6	8.0	7.2
Craftsworker	30.9	7.1	12.0	10.4
Operative	28.7	55.1	61.0	72.0

	Black Belt LMA		
Prof/Tech/Man	32.8	10.2	22.9	3.6
Sales/Clerical	14.5	45.6	6.3	30.3
Service Worker	2.3	1.1	--	3.6
Craftsworker	33.6	4.5	22.9	8.9
Operative	16.8	38.6	47.9	53.6

Source: U.S. Census of Population, 1980, PUMSD.

the other side are the full-time, capital intensive, larger-than-family operations.

The structure of agriculture and the nature of agricultural employment varies considerably across LMA groups. The data in Table 4.11, for example, show that the percentage of part-time farmers is highest in the large and mid-size urban LMAs, where over 60 percent of the farmers are so classified, and lowest in the black belt LMAs, where only 45.3 percent of the farmers are part-time producers. This is not surprising, since opportunities to combine farming with off-farm employment are more plentiful in and around larger metropolitan places.[13] Not unexpectedly, earnings from farming are higher for full-time farmers than for part-time farmers, regardless of LMA group. Farm income accounts for between 10.1 and 12.5 percent of total income for part-time farmers in the South. However, both total income and farm income for part-time farmers are highest in the large urban LMAs and lowest in the rural LMAs. The average earnings in 1980 for part-time producers in the large urban LMAs was $23,213, while the typical part-time farmers in a rural LMA earned only $17,357. A similar pattern is evident for full-time farmers. Farm income for this group is highest in the large urban LMAs ($14,225) and lowest in the rural LMAs ($11,386).

Selected characteristics of the production agriculture workforce are reported in Table 4.12. I have defined the production agriculture workforce as being composed of the following four groups: 1) full-time farmers (i.e., persons whose primary occupation is farmer, but who may hold a second job off of the farm); 2) part-time farmers (i.e., persons whose primary job is not farming, but who receive at least some income from farming); 3) farmworkers (i.e., persons whose primary occupation is working for wages on a farm); and 4) off-farm agricultural workers (i.e., farm foremen, nursery workers, groundskeepers, animal caretakers, etc.).

Clearly, production agriculture is one area of economic activity in which men predominate in all LMA groups. Further, it should be noted that the balance between hired farm labor, on the one hand, and full-time and part-time farming, on the other, varies across LMA groups. The black belt LMAs have the highest percentage (35.6 percent) of low-skilled, hired farmworkers. Not surprisingly, the bulk of these laborers are blacks. Black women are especially numerous in this occupational category. In fact, for black women in the production agriculture work force, the modal occupational category is farmworker in all LMA groups.

In the large urban LMAs, the percentage of full-time farmers is lowest (16.9 percent), while the percentage of off-farm agricultural workers is highest (36.1 percent). In the rural LMAs, the percentage of full-time and part-time farmers is highest, while the percentage of unskilled farmworkers is lowest. It is worth noting that the percentage of off-farm agricultural workers declines as one moves from the large, mid-size, and small urban LMAs to the rural and black belt LMAs. In the black belt, for example, only 13.7 percent of all workers fall into this category.

To conclude this examination of the agricultural workforce, let us turn to employment patterns in the agribusiness sector of the economy. Agribusiness is defined here as the agricultural services, food, and tobacco industries. The data in Table 4.12 show that agribusiness employment is a more important source of jobs in the rural and black belt LMAs and less important in the urban LMAs. Furthermore, not only does agribusiness employment represent a larger share of total employment in the rural and black belt LMAs, but this share appears to be growing larger vis-à-vis the large, mid-size, and small urban LMAs. Agribusiness employment, for example, grew by 31.4 percent in the black belt LMAs and by 28.3 percent in the rural LMAs between 1975 and 1984. In the large urban LMAs, on the other hand, agribusiness employment grew by less than one percent during this period.

This pattern of uneven growth is important when one realizes that average earnings for workers in the agribusiness sector are below the average manufacturing wage in all LMAs. Not surprisingly, given the patterning of inequalities across LMA groups, agribusiness workers earn less in the black belt and rural LMAs than in the urban LMAs. The average black belt worker, for example, earns only 65.7 percent as much as his/her counterpart in the large urban LMAs.

CONCLUSIONS

What I have attempted to show in this chapter is that the patterning of industrial development that has taken place across the South over the past 25 years has been uneven. The industries that pay the

Table 4.11
Distribution of Full-Time and Part-Time Farmers and Income From Farm and Non-Farm Sources by LMA Group

	Urban			Rural	Black Belt
	Large	Mid-Size	Small		
Part-Time Farmers					
% of All Farmers	60.1	61.0	57.2	57.0	45.3
Farm Earnings $	2,894	1,843	1,946	1,819	2,068
Total Earnings $	23,213	18,293	18,306	17,357	18,336
Full-Time Farmers					
% of All Farmers	39.9	39.0	42.8	43.0	54.7
Farm Earnings $	9,607	7,135	9,504	7,047	9,541
Total Earnings $	14,225	10,967	13,228	11,386	14,230

Source: U.S. Census of Population, 1980, PUMSD.

highest wages and that afford the most favorable occupational opportunities are disproportionately concentrated in the larger urban labor markets of the region. Transportation and electrical equipment manufacturing, for instance, are two of the highest wage industries in the South. In the mid-1980s, these two industries accounted for over one in four manufacturing jobs in the large urban LMAs and between 1975 and 1984 almost 65 percent of all new manufacturing growth in the large urban LMAs took place in these industries.

On the other hand, the lowest wage manufacturing industries, textile and apparel, accounted for less than eight percent of all manufacturing employment in the large urban LMAs and between 1975 and 1984 employment in these industries declined by 7000 workers. In the black belt, over one in four manufacturing workers is employed in the textile and apparel sector, while over one in five workers in the rural LMAs is affiliated with the textile and apparel industries. Compounding this problem, between 1975 and 1984, one in six new manufacturing jobs in the rural LMAs and one in five in the black belt were captured by these low-wage industries.

A similar pattern is evident for service industries as well. The highest wage service industries and those with the most favorable occupational structures, are concentrated in the urban LMAs of the South. The rural and black belt LMAs, on the other hand, are not only saddled with a disproportionately large share of low-wage service industries (e.g., retail trade, hospitality, etc.), but between 1975 and 1984 these low-wage services accounted for a larger share of service sector employment growth than they did in the urban LMAs. From a social justice perspective, it is difficult to see how the gaps between the rural and urban South in per capita income and other quality of life measures can be expected to close when the industrial development process is working to exacerbate structural inequalities among LMAs.

In this chapter I also explored the pervasiveness of race and sex segregation in the southern economy. The results here were consistent with what others have noted, namely that women and blacks are concentrated in the lowest wage, least prestigious positions in the occupational structure.[14] This patterning of differential occupational allocation holds across virtually all industrial sectors as well as LMA groups. Furthermore, not only are race and sex disparities evident within LMA groups, but there are important LMA group effects as well. Women and blacks, in general, fare better in the urban LMAs, particularly the large urban LMAs, in the region than they do in the

Table 4.12
Occupational Characteristics of the Production Agriculture Labor Force by Race, Sex, and LMA Group

Occupation	Large Urban LMA				
	White Male %	White Female %	Black Male %	Black Female %	All %
Full-Time Farmer	20.3	17.4	5.6	8.7	16.9
Part-Time Farmer	30.4	24.1	4.5	6.3	24.1
Farm Worker (on-farm)	15.1	25.4	39.5	58.7	22.9
Agricultural Worker (off-farm)	34.2	33.1	50.4	26.3	36.1
	Mid-Size Urban LMA				
Full-Time Farmer	32.1	22.7	19.8	13.7	27.9
Part-Time Farmer	33.3	35.7	8.6	15.8	19.2
Farm Worker (on-farm)	14.7	26.6	32.5	57.6	21.4
Agricultural Worker (off-farm)	19.9	15.0	39.1	12.9	21.5

				Small Urban LMA	
Full-Time Farmer	33.9	25.6	15.7	11.2	29.0
Part-Time Farmer	31.9	35.2	6.5	7.3	27.1
Farm Worker (on-farm)	16.4	23.6	46.2	64.9	24.2
Agricultural Worker (off-farm)	17.8	15.6	31.6	16.6	19.7
			Rural LMA		
Full-Time Farmer	35.4	33.4	20.6	19.6	33.6
Part-Time Farmer	33.4	25.6	5.7	9.8	29.4
Farm Worker (on-farm)	16.7	28.2	42.9	63.0	21.7
Agricultural Worker (off-farm)	14.5	12.8	30.8	7.6	16.3
			Black Belt LMA		
Full-Time Farmer	45.7	34.8	19.9	11.6	32.2
Part-Time Farmer	27.4	33.3	6.5	6.3	18.5
Farm Worker (on-farm)	15.6	20.3	54.7	72.6	35.6
Agricultural Worker (off-farm)	11.3	11.6	18.9	9.5	13.7

Source: U.S. Census of Population, 1980, PUMSD.

Table 4.13
Changes in Agribusiness Employment Between 1975 and 1984 and Average Worker Earnings by LMA Group

	Urban			Rural	Black Belt
	Large	Mid-Size	Small		
Agribusiness Employment					
1975	98,834	105,381	148,495	64,725	17,809
1984	99,392	118,102	168,010	83,038	23,409
Δ	558	12,721	19,515	18,313	5,600
Δ%	.6	12.1	13.1	28.3	31.4
Average Earnings ($)	9,648	9,233	8,024	7,332	6,344

Source: County Business Patterns, 1975 and 1984.

rural and black belt LMAs. No doubt the ability of blacks and women to secure more favorable occupational positions in the urban areas of the South is tied to the fact that these areas have an occupational mix characterized by a plethora of higher wage, white collar jobs.

One of the primary purposes of the de facto industrial policy strategy discussed in Chapter 1 is to create jobs. The data presented in this chapter indicate that local labor markets in the South have been quite successful in this endeavor. However, while creating jobs for southern workers has been a cornerstone of economic development policy in the region, attention to the "types" of jobs that have been created and the distribution of these jobs across race, sex, and LMA groups has received far less attention. Thus, for example, whether the new jobs that came into the region paid high wages or low wages, or whether they were equally accessible to whites/blacks or men/women has been neglected when the economic development policies were formulated and implemented.

The findings in this chapter provide further evidence that rural areas are diverging from urban areas in the South. Unlike the findings in Chapters 2 and 3, however, some reasons for this movement away from convergence are clearly evident here. Urban labor markets in the South have been able to shed many of their low-wage jobs while at the same time attracting a large number of high-wage positions. Rural areas, on the other hand, have attracted some high-wage employment, but these gains have been overshadowed by a greater influx of low-wage and low skill positions. Clearly, this type of industrial development can only lead to a lowering of the quality of life in rural areas of the South and the promise of even greater disparity in the standard of living and quality of life for residents in the urban and rural labor markets of the region.

NOTES

1. Naylor, Thomas A., and James Clotfelter, 1975. *Strategies for Change in the South* (Chapel Hill: University of North Carolina Press), p. 51.

2. Haren, Claude C., and Ronald W. Holling, 1979, "Industrial Development in Nonmetropolitan America: A Locational Perspective," in R. E. Lonsdale and H. L. Seyler (eds.), *Nonmetropolitan Industrialization* (New York: V. H. Winston and Sons), pp. 13-45.

3. Falk, William W., and Thomas A. Lyson, 1988, *High-Tech, Low-Tech, No-Tech: Recent Occupational and Industrial Changes in the South* (Albany: SUNY-Albany Press).

4. Thompson, Wilbur R., 1969, "The Economic Base of Urban Problems," in Neil W. Chamberlain (ed.), *Contemporary Economic Issues* (Homewood, IL: Richard D. Irwin), pp. 1-47.

5. Personick, Valerie, 1985, "A Second Look at Industry Output and Employment Trends Through 1995," *Monthly Labor Review* 58 (November), pp. 12-19.

6. Bloomquist, Leonard E., 1987, "Performance of the Rural Manufacturing Sector," in *Rural Economic Development in the 1980s: Preparing for the Future*, Agriculture and Rural Economy Division, Economic Research Service, U.S. Department of Agriculture. ERS Staff Report No. AGES870724, pp. 3-1-3-33.

7. For a similar treatment of the high technology sector of the economy, see Falk and Lyson, *High-Tech, Low-Tech*, especially Chapter 2.

8. Bloomquist, "Performance."

9. See, for example, Thomas A. Lyson, 1985, "Race and Sex Segregation in the Occupational Structure of Southern Employers," *Social Science Quarterly* 66(2): 281-295. Also, Paula England, 1981, "Assessing Trends in Occupational Sex Segregation, 1900-1976," in Ivar Berg (ed.), *Sociological Perspectives on Labor Markets* (New York: Academic Press), pp. 273-96.

10. Falk and Lyson, *High-Tech, Low-Tech*.

11. John E. Lee, 1983, "Some Consequences of the New Reality in U.S. Agriculture," in D. E. Brewster, W. D. Rasmussen, and G. Youngberg (eds.), *Farms in Transition* (Ames, Iowa: Iowa State University Press), pp. 3-22.

12. Lyson, Thomas A., and Georganne McMillin, 1986, *The Changing Structure of South Carolina Agriculture Since 1959*, Bulletin 655, South Carolina Agricultural Experiment Station (Clemson, SC: Clemson University).

13. Lyson, Thomas A., 1986, "Entry into Farming: Implications of a Dual Agricultural Structure," in J. J. Molnar (ed.), *Agricultural Change: Consequences for Southern Farms and Rural Communities* (Boulder, CO: Westview), pp. 155-76.

14. England, "Assessing Trends."

5. *Wedding Economic Development to Social Justice*

> The notion that social justice must be sacrificed for the sake of economic growth is simply wrong. Social justice is not a luxury bought at the expense of national economic health. It is the means for achieving and maintaining prosperity.[1]

During the decade of the 1970s, after a sustained period of impressive economic expansion, the pace of industrial development in the rural South began to slow. One consequence of this economic slowdown was that persons living in many rural areas of the sunbelt saw their standard of living begin to slip relative to their counterparts who lived in the more urban places of the South. Although both rural and urban areas experienced a tremendous influx of jobs across the industrial spectrum in the 1970s, the major metropolitan centers of the South clearly outpaced the remainder of the region. Not only did these places add more jobs than rural areas, but they attracted more "good" jobs—those offering high wages, lucrative fringe benefits, and high prestige. Consequently, one of the reasons why the urban South was able to improve its standing vis-à-vis the rural and black belt areas since the late 1970s was due to the booming sunbelt cities.[2]

At present, in the late 1980s, many rural and black belt LMAs in the South find themselves in very vulnerable economic positions. Many of the manufacturing industries that had moved to the South to escape the high wage, unionized North have begun to bypass the sunbelt and are shifting their production facilities directly to Third World countries. Unemployment rates in many rural and black belt counties rose to double digit levels during the 1981/82 recession and in many instances have yet to return to pre-recession levels. Poverty levels also rose after the recession to the extent that there are more people living in poverty today in these places than there were in 1970. And as the data in Chapter 3 showed, compounding these problems is a woefully deficient stock of human capital and an understaffed and underfunded infrastructure in the rural and black belt South.

To understand how the standard of living and quality of life in the urban LMAs of the South improved relative to the rural and black belt LMAs, I turned to the sets of state and local policies and programs that guided economic development efforts in the region. De facto industrial policies rest on the notion that economic development is a contest that pits one locality against another for new jobs. It is my belief that in this contest rural communities are placed in a "no win" situation. They are forced to offer lucrative business incentives such as tax breaks, subsidized loans, and gifts of land and buildings with only faint hope that they will be able to attract any employer.

The shortsightedness of this approach to economic development is slowly and often grudgingly being acknowledged by industrial recruiters in the region. The Southern Growth Policies Board, the Ford Foundation, and others have begun to document what happens to small rural communities that get caught up in the recruiting wars.[3] The following example is excerpted from a 1986 Ford Foundation study, *Shadows in the Sunbelt*:

> Consider, for instance, one rural county in southern Georgia where local leaders joined together in early 1984 to offset the lagging growth in jobs and economic activity which was stunting the local tax base. After consulting with the State Department of Industry and Trade, the group raised $500,000 to hire a professional recruiter and finance construction of a new plant facility for the recruiter to fill.
>
> Two years later, their considerable efforts have netted no new industries, no new jobs and no firm prospects. And the county has found new competition from an adjoining county where a major plant closing idled 2000 workers and left an expanse of low cost industrial floor space. Yet county leaders still see the best hope for their economy in plant location decisions that will be made from afar. (p. 11)[4]

In a somewhat different vein, the residents of Westmorland, Pennsylvania, have an unsettling message to send to their southern neighbors about the dangers of industrial giveaways. To attract a large Volkswagen assembly plant into the region in 1976, the state of Pennsylvania assembled a package of state and local subsidies valued at $150 million (or close to $300 million in 1988 dollars). The key lure was a $40 million loan at 1.7 percent interest that VW did not have to begin repaying until 1998. Volkswagen accepted the offer and began manufacturing Volkswagen Rabbits/Golfs in Westmorland. In November 1987, citing lack of sales, Volkswagen announced that it was closing the plant and that 2500 workers at the facility would lose their jobs. According to David Osborne, author of *The Next Agenda*, a book on state economic development, "It's a classic example of why smokestack chasing doesn't work. You're just bringing in a plant, not a process of growth."[5]

The economic chaos caused by the oil shocks of 1973 and 1978 and the deep recession in 1981/82 brought about a call for a national industrial policy. Several books and countless articles debated the merits of such a policy.[6] After the 1981/82 recession, however, the call for a national industrial policy quickly faded as the economy entered a period of sustained economic growth. By the late 1980s, the industrial policy question had moved far off centerstage and was replaced by an economic policy agenda that emphasized "revitalizing" American industry and enhancing the "competitiveness" of American-made products both at home and overseas. The major social and economic upheavals that filled the pages of the nation's newspapers and television screens in the early 1980s were quickly forgotten.

Looked at in total, the American economy seems to have made a magnificent rebound from the doom and gloom days of the early 1980s. Beneath the veneer of aggregate statistics, however, there lurks another story. Wealthy individuals and well-to-do communities have prospered in recent years. The Northeast and Southwest, for example, continue to outdistance the rest of the country in economic growth. During the same period, however, those people and places at the bottom of the socioeconomic ladder have seen their situation erode even further. Stagnating conditions in the rural South represent a sharp contrast to the upbeat mood in other regions of the country.

Barry Bluestone, Bennett Harrison, and Lester Thurow were some of the first observers to note the growing polarity between rich and poor in this country and the decline of the middle class. Bluestone and Harrison, for example, recently showed that 41 percent of all new jobs generated between 1979 and 1985 were in the low-wage category, while Thurow revealed that both income inequality and the concentration of wealth have been increasing in the United States in recent years.[7] Writing for the *New York Times* in 1986, Ravi Batra, an economist at Southern Methodist University, noted: "During the past six years, President Reagan's policy of creating affluence through inequality has indeed enriched the rich, but only showered misery on the poor. There has been a trickle down of poverty."[8]

In this book, I have attempted to show that the disparity between the haves and have-nots has a geographic focus. People living in rural and black belt areas of the South have seen their living standards and economic opportunities steadily deteriorate vis-à-vis their more urban neighbors in the region. The rising economic tide of the mid- and late 1980s has not lifted all boats.

THE RURAL SOUTH IN CRISIS

At this point in time, state and local leaders in the South are aware that rural areas need immediate and long-term attention. But it is my impression that despite a great deal of rhetoric, concrete, workable plans are lacking. Instead, state legislatures in the region have responded to the rural crisis with vague and often ill-defined programs and initiatives. Stuart Rosenfeld, director of research for the Southern Growth Policies Board, recently enumerated the ways in which various southern states are responding to calls of rural distress:

> In 1987, the Georgia legislature passed the Rural Economic Development Law "to provide a program of rural economic development" to rural counties where the per capita income is less than 70 percent of the national average or where the unemployment rate is more than 35 percent above the state average. (Virtually all rural Georgia counties fall into one or the other of these categories.)
>
> Arkansas recently passed legislation directing the state's industrial development commission to form advisory teams to coordinate rural development. (This is the same state that made smokestack chasing an endurance contest when they made 60,000 phone calls in the 1960s in search of new industrial prospects.)

In Mississippi, a comprehensive economic development plan was formulated that specifies special programs "for rural areas of the state and those areas with the highest unemployment and lowest per capita income." (Mississippi has *no* counties in which per capita income is at the national average.)

In 1987, the Advisory Committee on the Future of the Florida Legislature recommended that the governor, the Speaker and the President of the Senate appoint "a study committee of public and private sector members to develop strategies to assist rural Florida in providing short and long term economic development opportunities and needed infrastructure, including education and health facilities."

In South Carolina, the state Development Board recently created a new position, Assistant to the Director for Rural Development. The responsibilities of that position include establishing a program to counsel, advise and assist rural places to stimulate economic development.[9]

Even the most concerned and sympathetic observer would be hard pressed to believe that any of these initiatives will have any lasting, or even short-term, benefits.

A more ambitious, although less well-defined, set of goals for the rural South was put forth in 1986 by the Commission on the Future of the South, in their report, "Halfway Home And a Long Way to Go." The explicit charge of the Commission was to "produce a short readable report to the people of the South which can be used by governors, legislators, and other leaders to mobilize support for those public policies and public–private partnerships which will increase per capita income, reduce poverty, and reduce unemployment for Southerners by 1992."[10] The ten regional objectives they enumerated included: 1) providing a nationally competitive education for all southern students; 2) mobilizing resources to eliminate adult functional illiteracy; 3) preparing a flexible, globally competitive workforce; 4) strengthening society as a whole by strengthening at-risk families; 5) increasing the economic development role of higher education; 6) increasing the region's capacity to generate and use technology; 7) implementing new economic development strategies aimed at home grown business and industry; 8) enhancing the region's natural and cultural resources; 9) developing pragmatic leaders with a global vision; and 10) improving the structure and performance of local governments.

Because of the scope and the implications of these objectives for social policy, they merit careful scrutiny and discussion by all persons concerned about the future of the South. However, like the initiatives put forth in various southern states, it is unclear exactly how these objectives will be operationalized or how they will be achieved.

TOWARD THE FUTURE

The rhetoric of economic development in the South has historically been filled with calls for "fresh ideas" and "innovative programs." These phrases no doubt seem trite to long-term observers of the rural development scene in the South. A region whose economic and political leaders who for so long prided themselves on obtaining high rankings on various and sundry "business climate" indices are finding it difficult to do anything about the low taxes, low wages, unregulated environment, and mediocre schools that yielded that high ranking. But unless the rural and black belt areas of the South wish to fall further behind, it is time to move beyond the de facto and ultimately self-defeating economic development policies of the past.

It is becoming abundantly clear that the so-called free market, supply-side macroeconomic policies that guided economic development initiatives in the United States during the 1980s have generally exacerbated the economic woes of families and communities in the rural South. The Reagan administration's stance toward rural development could best be described as one of "benign neglect." According to a recent report by the Office of Technology Assessment, "This policy of 'benign neglect' is based on the view that rural communities have strong, cohesive, social institutions and can help themselves better than the Federal Government and State Government can." The report continues, "There is strong evidence that many, if not most, rural communities have suffered a decline in their strength, cohesion and capabilities and are now much less able to help themselves."[11]

As the data in Table 5.1 indicate, the decline in federal aid programs to rural America has been nothing short of remarkable during the 1980s. In 1980, the federal government pumped nearly $10 billion into rural America, including nearly $7 billion in General Revenue Sharing. By 1987, the federal government was giving less than $1.2 billion to rural America and General Revenue Sharing funds had been cut to zero. Tom Murphy, Speaker of the Georgia House of

Table 5.1
Decline in Federal Aid Programs to Rural America in Millions of Dollars: 1980-1987

Agency	1980	1981	1982	1983	1984	1985	1986	1987
Economic Dev. Administration	$ 532	$ 378	$ 197	$ 316	$ 258	$ 226	$ 167	$ 180
FmHA Business Loans	1074	741	300	300	300	61	96	96
Com. Development Block Grant	1159	1109	1037	1037	1040	1040	897	900
General Revenue Sharing	6850	4600	4567	4567	4567	4567	4050	0
Total	$9615	$6828	$6101	$6220	$6165	$5894	$5210	$1176

Source: National Association of Development Organizations, 1987.

Representatives, summarized the sentiments of many state and local policymakers when he recently noted, "The federal government has just about destroyed economic development in rural areas. They've taken all the tools away."[12]

It is my observation that a strong federal role is essential if we hope to reverse the discouraging social and economic trends in the rural and black belt South. I am not alone in the belief that the federal government has an important role to play in future economic development efforts and in ensuring that social justice is served by these efforts. The National Conference of Catholic Bishops, in their 1986 report "Economic Justice for All,"[13] for example, highlighted the moral function of government to protect human rights and secure "basic justice for all members of the commonwealth." The Bishops further stated that "full employment is the foundation of a just economy" and noted that the government has an important role to play in creating jobs.[14]

Kenneth Wilkinson, a community development specialist at Penn State University and a former president of the Rural Sociological Society, notes that the United States ". . . cannot simply turn the task of rural development over to the rural communities with confidence that local action will solve our pressing rural problems."[15] Instead, Wilkinson believes that a two-fold attack that combines federal initiatives with local initiatives is needed. The federal government must provide the leadership and resources to enhance the social and economic well-being of rural residents.[16]

Despite a national political agenda that has favored less, not more, federal intervention in recent years into helping to solve the problems of America's underclass, there is at least some support among legislators and policymakers in Washington for reinvigorating the federal role in economic development matters. A recent book edited by Representative David Obey (D.-Wisconsin) and Senator Paul Sarbanes (D.-Maryland), *The Changing American Economy*, argues that it is foolish to insist that the benefits of economic growth and efficiency cannot be distributed equitably across different groups and regions of the country. A number of contributors to this book call for "a renewed period of policy creativity that will accomplish for this generation what the GI Bill of Rights, the National Defense Education Act, and many other programs did for the last—create new opportunities for individuals to better themselves and in the process the nation at large."[17]

Advocating that the federal government take a more active stance in rural development efforts does not mean that states and local communities have no role to play. For instance, most economic development policies should be carried out to a large extent through state agencies and programs. Only states can adequately coordinate different interest groups and opportunities within their boundaries. Furthermore, local economic development strategies that are politically feasible cannot be imposed by the federal government. Finally, state governments can best implement programs within the broad policy guidelines of the federal government to ensure that the most needy rural residents and communities are served.[18]

Local governments and agencies must work within national and state guidelines and priorities, but they should have a great deal of flexibility to tailor initiatives to local conditions and resources. It is at the local level that services are delivered and programs administered to improve the quality of life of those on the bottom of the socioeconomic ladder. As the Office of Technology Assessment report notes, "Local governments and agencies are capable of developing more diversity in sources of funding and types of services that are delivered. Localities are better able to identify and use particular local resources in the process of development."[19]

Nevertheless, if we accept the premise of greater federal involvement in rural economic development, the question becomes what types of programs and policies would best assist those at the bottom of the socioeconomic ladder? There are three distinct components to a federally sponsored rural economic development program. These are: 1) human resource development programs to improve the skills and abilities of the labor force; 2) infrastructure programs to improve the provision and delivery of social and business services in rural areas; and 3) equity and justice programs to enhance the opportunity structure for those at the bottom.

HUMAN RESOURCE DEVELOPMENT

Economic development specialists and policymakers are in almost total agreement that an integral part of any rural development effort is a program to prepare workers for jobs in a changing economy. As Ray Marshall, former secretary of Labor in the Carter administration, noted a decade and half ago, "It is difficult to conceive of an effective rural development strategy that would not contain a sizeable manpower component, whether that strategy were designed to facilitate the adjustment of people from declining industries to growth sectors or areas, to relocate people from labor surplus areas, to facilitate economic development, or to create public service jobs for those not likely to be absorbed in the private sector or those not likely to benefit from relocation."[20]

Today, these same sentiments are once again being voiced by academicians and policymakers alike. As Brady Deaton, an agricultural economist at Virginia Polytechnical Institute and his colleagues recently noted: "Human resource development is receiving renewed attention in the South today as its role in the region's economic future is reassessed. The resurgence of interest in this area has come ... from Southern leaders themselves who are impatient with the unmet needs in education and training, health care, and social services that have too frequently been eclipsed in the build-up of the region's infrastructure."[21]

Despite the inherent logic of a coherent human resource development component to economic growth strategies, the dominant political mood in Washington, since at least 1980, has been to downplay these types of efforts. George Gilder, author of *Wealth and Poverty*, expressed the sentiments of the Reagan administration when he wrote, "Like welfare, CETA [then the major public employment and training program] often has the effect of sheltering people from the realities of their lives and thus prevents them from growing up and finding or creating useful tasks."[22] Not surprisingly, under the Reagan administration, labor market and human resource development programs have been drastically curtailed.

The Comprehensive Employment Training Act (CETA), for example, was replaced by the Job Training Partnership Act (JTPA) in 1982. CETA was designed as a coordinating mechanism for the various and sundry state and local programs that had mushroomed in the 1960s under the aegis of the Manpower Development Training Act. The effectiveness of CETA is unclear, even today. However, a recent report by Elizabeth Evanson for the University of Wisconsin's Institute for Research on Poverty notes that CETA programs did increase employment in the short run, when the economy was sluggish. Further, CETA was successful in reallocating employment toward disadvantaged groups.[23]

JTPA, on the other hand, is characterized by decentralized admintration, emphasis on the private sector, and a focus limited to job training for poor youth and permanently displaced workers. There is *no* public service employment under JTPA. Although it may be too early to evaluate the effectiveness of JTPA in the rural South, the fact that this program relies more on local initiatives and creates no new jobs suggests that it will have minimal effect on reducing unemployment and underemployment or in raising the skill levels of workers in the region. As Brian Rungeling and his colleagues have noted, ". . . the plain fact is that most rural governments are incapable of administering human resource programs. The problem is more pervasive than simply lack of staff and expertise. Too often there is a vested interest in rural areas of the South that is hostile to change. Rural governments are too concerned with maintaining the status quo."[24]

Beyond the issue of how JTPA is administered is the level of funding for JTPA generally and the ability of rural areas of the South to compete for the resources that are available. A recent report by the Economic Research Service of the U.S. Department of Agriculture notes that current funding for JTPA is only 40 percent of the $10 billion allocated to CETA in its peak year (1979). Equally distressing, a Government Accounting Office (GAO) analysis states that underestimates of unemployment in rural areas may have cost nonmetropolitan counties as much as $129 million in lost JTPA funds in 1984.[25]

The economic plight of rural and black belt LMAs and the growing divergence between the rural and urban South on a broad range of social indicators that I have documented in Chapters 2-4 suggest that we need more, not less, federal attention in the region. The rural and black belt areas are no longer able to attract branch plants to supplement or replace agricultural jobs. Instead, they must depend heavily on small business growth, entrepreneurship, and service industries. Unfortunately, this is a challenge that is hardly addressed at all by the federal government.

George Autry, president of MDC, Inc., a private, nonprofit research corporation concerned with employment policies and programs in the South, highlighted the problems faced by the rural South today:

> Because of the geographic isolation of entrepreneurs and the high transaction costs for banks, there is insufficient capital in the forms we need

it in the rural South. And there are too few bankable ideas, and too little assistance available to fledgling businesses.[26]

Given that the declining economic base in manufacturing and agriculture is the unintended byproduct of federal policy, Autry asks, "... could we not help rebuild that base with industrial policy interventions?"[27] In particular, he calls for the federal government to foster seed and venture capital funds and to encourage technical assistance in packaging loans and in building small businesses.

Over and above the need to nurture small business growth and stimulate the entrepreneurial spirit, federal attention must be directed toward the technical and vocational skills needed for the new economic ventures that will replace the textile mills and branch manufacturing plants. Stuart Rosenfeld calls for a type of "generic" vocational training that inculcates a set of basic industrial skills and behaviors related to independence and responsibility. Ideally, these skills would be combined with on-the-job training or apprenticeship programs where the more technical and industry specific skills would be acquired.[28] Echoing these sentiments, the Southern Growth Policies Board in their 1985 report, "Looking Forward: Visions of the Future of the South," called for education and training policies that prepare workers for life-long adaptability in a fast changing job market and training programs to upgrade skills and retrain workers.[29]

Apart from these programs, there is merit in William Wilson's proposal "... to devise a national labor-market strategy to insure adaptability of the labor force to changing employment opportunities."[30] He calls for a refocusing of attention away from "remedial programs in the public sector for the poor and unemployed" and toward programs that would match skills and talents to opportunities in the private sector. Wilson makes the interesting and important point that to draw sustained political support for a program of economic reform, "... it is necessary that training or retraining, transitional employment benefits, and relocation assistance be available to all members of society who choose to use them...."[31]

In sum, it is time to realize that the human resource problems of the rural and black belt South demand attention at the federal level. Without a strong federal presence in rural economic development, the rural and black belt areas are destined to fall even further behind the rest of the country. The Southern Growth Policies Board notes what is likely to happen if we continue down the same path of minimal federal involvement in human resource development issues.

> The long-range goal of the New Federalism is to eliminate federal funding for many human resource and economic development programs by shifting program and financing responsibilities back to the state and local levels. Advocates of New Federalism would provide alternative funding through federal relinquishment or sharing of various tax instruments (such as excise taxes) and through reducing federal income taxes. However, if the federal tax burden is diminished, voting patterns suggest that fiscally conservative southern voters will resist making up for lost revenues by raising state taxes. This will have serious consequences for the continued education reforms which are vital to the South's economic future.[32]

Infrastructure Development

The second component of an effective and socially just economic development policy for the rural South is infrastructure development. Public infrastructure is defined as the physical capital investments supported by the public sector to enhance the standard of living and quality of life of residents in particular labor market areas. Infrastructure also refers to the public facilities and equipment required to support private sector economic activity. Table 5.2 illustrates the broad categories of public infrastructure in the United States.

Even a cursory glance at the types of public service and production facilities listed in Table 5.2 suggests that remote places like the rural and black belt LMAs of the South lack many of the infrastructure amenities found in the more urban locales of the region. For instance, rural and black belt LMAs have fewer libraries, community recreation facilities, advanced telecommunication equipment (e.g., cable TV) than the more urban LMAs in the South. Likewise, rural and black belt areas lack intra- and inter-community transit as well as the levels of police and fire protection that are available to urban residents.

There is evidence to indicate that infrastructure investments are a precursor to economic development. The money spent for new roads, installation or expansion of water and sewer systems, school improvements, and the like are seen as necessary, although not necessarily sufficient, steps in stimulating economic development.[33] Clearly,

Table 5.2
Categories of Public Infrastructure

Service Facilities	Production Facilities
Education	**Energy**
Elementary Schools	Direct Power Suppliers
Middle Schools	
Secondary Schools	**Fire Safety**
Public Libraries	
	Fire Stations
Health	Vehicles
	Communications System
Hospitals	Water Supply and Storage
Nursing Home	
Ambulatory (Outpatient) Care Facilities	**Solid Waste**
Ambulatory Dental Care Facilities	Collection Facilities and Equipment
Ambulatory Mental Health Facilities	Disposal Sites
Residential Facilities for:	**Telecommunications**
--Orphans and dependent children	
--the emotionally disturbed	Cable Television
--alcoholics and drug abusers	Over-The-Air Televison
--the physically handicapped	Disaster Preparedness
--mentally retarded	
--blind and deaf	**Waste Water**
Emergency Vehicle Service	
	Sewer Mains and Collection Systems
Justice	Treatment and Disposal Systems
Law Enforcement Facilities	
Jails	**Water Supply**
Recreation	Community Systems
	--Storage Facilities
Community Recreation Facilities	--Treatment Facilities
	--Delivery Facilities
Transportation	On-Site Wells and Cisterns
Railroad Facilities	
Airport and Related Facilities	
Streets and Highways (including bridges)	
Inter- and Intra-Community Transit	

Source: Abt Associates, <u>National Rural Community Facilities Assessment Study: Pilot Phase, Final Report</u>, March, 1980, p. 16.

most firms, and especially manufacturing plants, must have access to roads, rail lines, water and sewer systems, and other necessities. Without an adequate infrastructure base, localities have little hope of developing their economies.

In recent years, researchers and policymakers have begun to pay close attention to the condition of the nation's infrastructure. A study written by Pat Choate and Susan Walter, *America in Ruins: The Decaying Infrastructure*, highlighted the deficiencies and gaps in the nation's infrastructure. With respect to rural infrastructure needs, the authors note that virtually nothing is known about the provision of basic services and the adequacy of existing facilities in nonmetropolitan America.[34] Even a recent study by the Economic Research Service of the U.S. Department of Agriculture has been able to shed relatively little light on the matter.[35]

Nevertheless, as William Fox recently noted, "... a basic infrastructure is necessary to support most private sector production: electricity, water, communications, and certain transportation modes, such as roads. These are necessary supply-side inputs to business operations, though the need for such infrastructure varies widely by firm. Without this infrastructure, rural communities could not grow and compete for new jobs, and firms would be unable to expand."[36]

The federal government has historically supported infrastructure development through direct expenditures, grants, loans, and loan guarantees. However, in recent years, the new federalism proposals of the Reagan administration have resulted in a scaling back of federal support for infrastructure development. State and local governments, in turn, have had to assume responsibility for the financing and delivery of many infrastructure functions.[37]

For the already economically marginal communities in the South, especially those in the rural and black belt LMAs, the new federalism as it applies to building and maintaining infrastructure, places these localities in a particularly disadvantaged position vis-à-vis more affluent northern and urban areas. Without federal funds to subsidize infrastructure development, it is difficult to see how a socioeconomic environment conducive to establishing and sustaining a strong economic base can be created. By cutting federal support for infrastructure projects and turning over this responsibility to state and local governments will surely exacerbate existing inequalities between the rural and urban South.

It is my view that, as was the case with human resource development programs, the federal government has a vital role to play in planning, financing, and maintaining the nation's infrastructure. I am particularly sympathetic with a proposal put forth by Pat Choate and Susan Walter that calls on the federal government to establish a national public works investment policy and a supporting capital budget. According to these authors, "A national capital budget could bring new coherence to public works policymaking and program management by providing a framework for legislative and administrative decisions."[38] The ultimate goals of such a policy would be to specify and meet basic levels of public works services and facilities for specific populations and geographic areas and to specify the extent to which the public sector should finance infrastructure to support economic development. Among other things, a national capital budget would provide a framework for analyzing the social and equity issues associated with the distribution of public works funds within and among various regions.[39]

For households and communities in the rural and black belt South, a national capital budget could ensure the presence of at least some minimal level of infrastructure necessary to stimulate development. Many localities in the South lack the economic base to finance the development of an infrastructure that can meet both the personal needs of the local citizenry (e.g., schools, healthcare facilities, etc.) and at the same time establish and maintain services and facilities needed to attract new industry. A federally coordinated capital budget in concert with policies and programs to develop and enhance human resources in the South would go a long way toward reducing the inequities that have come to distinguish the urban from the rural South.

Equity and Justice Programs

There is a growing awareness that human resource development policies and infrastructure programs may be necessary to stimulate economic development. But these two sets of programs alone do not ensure that those people and communities resting on the bottom rungs of the socioeconomic ladder will be brought into the mainstream of American society. To be truly effective, human resource and infrastructure programs must operate in a social and political climate that guarantees everyone an adequate and decent standard of living and access to the means/resources/opportunities (e.g., jobs, welfare programs, etc.) to achieve this standard of living. A policy agenda to address these concerns would include, but not be limited to minimum wage legislation, full employment programs, and welfare reform.

Full Employment Programs

Full employment and minimum wage legislation are important cornerstones to an economic development strategy that could improve the lot of workers in the rural and black belt LMAs. With respect to a full employment policy, the original language of the Employment Act of 1946 proposed that every American should have the right to a job. Samuel Bowles, David Gordon, and Thomas Weisskopf spell out an "Economic Bill of Rights" in their recent book, *Beyond the Wasteland*, in which the "Right to a Decent Job" is their first concern. They propose that the federal government establish a goal of no more than two percent unemployment. When unemployment exceeds two percent in a local area, they call on the federal government to make funds available to local governments to finance public employment.[40]

In a somewhat different vein, Representative David Obey (D.-Wisconsin), chairman of the Joint Economic Committee of the U.S. Congress, recently noted that "the ability to provide work for all who want it is thus the key test of a society's ability to deliver on the promise of opportunity."[41] Obey acknowledges that the U.S. economy has created an impressive number of new jobs in the 1980s, but he adds that we have yet to reduce unemployment to full employment levels.[42] The bottom line is that the inability to deliver on the promise of full employment means that places like the rural and black belt LMAs are destined to remain areas in which a disproportionately large reserve army of the unemployed reside.

William J. Wilson, a noted sociologist at the University of Chicago, advocates a macroeconomic policy that would promote both economic growth and full employment. He notes that most ad hoc strategies to promote full employment ignore certain fundamental questions.

> The questions include the relative impact on labor markets in different areas of the country; the type, variety, and volume of jobs to be gener-

ated; the extent to which residents in low income neighborhoods will have access to these jobs; the quality of these jobs in terms of stability and pay; the extent to which proposed strategies enhance the employment opportunities of both new entrants into the labor market and the currently unemployed; and whether the benefits from economic development and employment provide reasonable returns on public investment.[43]

While Wilson's plan is designed to benefit all segments of society, his program has special appeal for stagnating and declining areas of the rural South. The profound structural changes that are reshaping the contours of the U.S. economy have adversely affected employment patterns in the rural South. The continuing demise of production agriculture coupled with the decline of employment in low-wage, low skill, peripheral manufacturing industries have left many rural and black belt LMAs with severe unemployment and underemployment problems. Certainly, a program designed to ameliorate the structural dislocations caused by plant closings, farm foreclosures, and other factors that affect employment levels such as technology, profit rates, unionization, and the like would go a long way toward enhancing the quality of life in the rural South.

Minimum Wage

Creating employment opportunities is only part of the solution to the problems plaguing the rural South. The jobs that are being created must pay a livable wage. In the mid-1980s, the minimum wage of $3.35 an hour translated into an annual income of less than $7,000 a year, which is less than the poverty threshold for a family of three. Although less than ten percent of all workers earn the minimum, industries and occupations that pay minimum wages represent a disproportionately large share of the jobs found in the rural and black belt South. Over half of all retail trade jobs (mostly sales clerks), for instance, earn the minimum wage. As I noted in Chapter 4, retail sales represents a larger part of the service economy in the rural and black belt LMAs than in the mid-size and large urban LMAs.

During the Reagan years, the minimum wage was raised only once, in 1981. At that time, the minimum wage was 46.2 percent of the average hourly wage in the United States and 41.9 percent of the average manufacturing wage. By 1987, the minimum wage had slipped to 37.3 percent of the average hourly wage and 33.8 percent of the average manufacturing wage.

Several proposals have been made to raise the minimum wage, including legislation introduced by Senator Edward Kennedy (D.-Mass.) and Representative Augustus Hawkins (D.-Calif.) to peg the minimum wage to the average national hourly wage. The Kennedy-Hawkins Bill would benefit workers in the rural South in at least two ways. First, it would establish a wage floor that would rise when the average national wage rose. This would ensure that the economic lot of southern workers would be tied to what happens to wages in the nation as a whole. Secondly, and related to this, the rural South would no longer be as attractive to footloose firms whose only motivation for setting up shop in the hinterlands of the sunbelt is to exploit the low-wage workforce.

Welfare Reform

The rural South, and especially black belt locales, have yet to participate fully in the social welfare programs in the United States. Many federal welfare programs that provide direct benefits to low income people are aimed at the needs and characteristics of the urban poor and lack sensitivity to the unique characteristics of the rural poor.[44]

The Aid to Families with Dependent Children (AFDC) program is a case in point. Although federal, state, and local governments share the costs of this program, payments vary from state to state along criteria established by the states themselves. In general, AFDC payments in predominantly rural, southern states are lower than benefits in the North, even though the cost of living in northern rural areas is not substantially different than that in the South. For example, a family of four in rural Mississippi receives less than half of the benefits available to a similar family in rural New York.

Furthermore, 23 AFDC programs, again mostly in the South, provide benefits only to female-headed households. Families with male heads are denied assistance. These eligibility criteria obviously discriminate against the rural poor in the South. In urban areas only about 40 percent of the poor families are headed by males, whereas in rural areas over 70 percent of the poor families have male heads. One solution to this problem would be to require all states to establish AFDC-UP (Unemployed Parent) programs. This reform would provide benefits to all poverty stricken two-parent families and clearly raise the benefits paid to the rural poor.[45]

Additionally, with the exception of only a few federal programs (Food Stamps, Earned Income Tax Credit, and states with AFDC-UP programs), families without children, single persons under 65, and working male-headed families are ineligible for federally sponsored public assistance. This works to the disadvantage of the rural South since there are proportionately more families with these characteristics than urban families.

A comprehensive welfare reform package that would equalize payments among states and extend coverage to groups that are now excluded would go a long way toward improving the economic life chances and standard of living for rural families in general, and rural black families in particular. The importance of welfare reform for rural areas was noted during the Carter administration when a White House Rural Development Background paper (*Social and Economic Trends in Rural America*) noted that "... welfare reform is a key element of federal rural policy. No other single policy action would have as immediate and obvious consequences for their [rural poor] well-being—in terms of their ability to obtain goods and services essential to a decent level of living."[46]

SOME FINAL OBSERVATIONS

The 1980s have not been good in many rural labor markets in the South. After decades of economic growth and a steadily improving standard of living, the 1980s have been a period of slow growth, stagnation, and even decline for many nonmetropolitan communities in the sunbelt. Ironically, the growing divergence between the rural and urban South has occurred during what has been widely touted by recent Republican administrations as the longest sustained economic recovery since World War II.

It has become clear that there are no quick fix solutions to the social and economic malaise in the rural South. The patchwork and piecemeal federal programs in the areas of human resource and infrastructure development that have replaced the more broadly based and concerted efforts of the 1960s and 1970s have done little to alleviate the structural inequalities that have come to separate rural from urban LMAs. Compounding the economic woes in the rural

South is an abrogation of responsibility by the federal government for the necessary leadership and financial resources to address these problems. The New Federalism policies of recent years have resulted in state and local governments taking on more responsibility for solving their own social and economic problems. Relatively prosperous and affluent states and communities have been able to adequately handle this task. Poor southern states and especially distressed communities in the rural and black belt areas of the region, on the other hand, have neither the resources nor the leadership necessary to keep them from falling further behind their more prosperous counterparts.

As America approaches the 1990s and the 21st century, it is time to acknowledge the shortcomings of existing de facto economic development policies. The economic development strategies born and refined in the South that turned economic development into a contest pitting state against state and community against community in the quest for jobs, need to be replaced. More just and equitable policies and programs that attempt to balance the benefits of national economic expansion across all groups of workers and all types of communities must be implemented. Without an overt concern for equity and justice issues, existing socioeconomic inequalities are destined to grow larger. A litmus test for future economic development programs should be how they affect the least well-off communities, those that are least able to pull themselves up by their own bootstraps.

NOTES

1. Reich, Robert, 1983, *The Next American Frontier* (New York: Times Books), p. 282.

2. See for example, George B. Autry, 1988, "Federal Neglect Crippling the Rural South," *Atlanta Journal/Constitution* (January 17).

3. Some of these reports include, "Halfway Home and a Long Way to Go" (Research Triangle Park, NC: Southern Growth Policies Board, 1986); "Shadows in the Sunbelt," A Report of the MDC Panel on Rural Economic Development, May 1986 (Chapel Hill, NC: MDC, Inc.).

4. *Shadows in the Sunbelt*, p. 11.

5. Beazley, J. Ernest, and Jacob M. Schlesinger, 1987; "Town Stunned by VW Plant's Closing Though End Had Been Long Expected," *Wall Street Journal* (November 23).

6. See, for example, Barry Bluestone and Bennett Harrison, 1982, *The Deindustrialization of America* (New York: Basic Books); Samuel Bowles, David M.

Gordon, and Thomas E. Weiskopf, 1983, *Beyond the Wasteland* (New York: Anchor/Doubleday); Felix Rohatyn, 1981, "Reconstructing America," *New York Review of Books*, (February 5); Robert Reich, 1982, "Making Industrial Policy," *Foreign Affairs* (Spring).

7. See Barry Bluestone and Bennett Harrison, 1987, "The Grim Truth About the Job Miracle," *New York Times* (February 1); Lester C. Thurow, 1987, "A Surge in Inequality," *Scientific American*, 236(5): 30-37.

8. Batra, Ravi, 1987, "An Ominous Trend to Greater Inequality," *New York Times* (May 3).

9. Rosenfeld, Stuart, 1988, "The Tale of Two Souths," in L. J. Beaulieu (ed.), *The Rural South in Crisis: Challenges for the Future* (Boulder, CO: Westview).

10. Southern Growth Policies Board, 1986, "Halfway Home and a Long Way to Go," p. 4.

11. Office of Technology Assessment, 1986, "Technology, Public Policy and the Changing Structure of Agriculture" (Washington, D.C.: U.S. Government Printing Office).

12. Quoted in Jim Auchmutey and Priscilla Painton, 1986, "Revenue Cutbacks Leave Region with a Thinner Thread of Hope," *Atlanta Constitution* (November 20).

13. National Conference of Catholic Bishops, 1986, *Economic Justice for All*, Publication No. 101 (Washington, D.C.: U.S. Catholic Conference, Inc.).

14. Ibid., p. 69.

15. Wilkinson, Kenneth P., 1984, "Implementing a National Strategy of Rural Development," *Rural Sociologist*, 4(5): 351.

16. Ibid.

17. Obey, David R., and Paul Sarbanes (eds.), 1986, *The Changing American Economy* (New York: Basil Blackwell), p. 5.

18. Office of Technology Assessment, 1986, "Technology, Public Policy and the Changing Structure of Agriculture," p. 246-247.

19. Ibid., p. 247.

20. Marshall, Ray, 1974, *Rural Workers in Rural Labor Markets* (Salt Lake City: Olympus Publishing Co.), p. 131.

21. Deaton, Brady J., and Anne S. Deaton, 1988, "Educational Reform and Regional Development," in Beaulieu (ed.), *The Rural South in Crisis*, pp. 304-24.

22. Gilder, George, 1981, *Wealth and Poverty* (New York: Basic Books), p. 190.

23. Evanson, Elizabeth, 1984, "Employment Programs for the Poor: Government in the Labor Market," *Focus* 7(3).

24. Rungeling, Brian, Lewis H. Smith, Vernon M. Briggs, Jr., and John F. Adams, 1977, *Employment, Income and Welfare in the Rural South* (New York: Praeger).

25. Ross, Peggy J., and Stuart A. Rosenfeld, 1987, "Human Resource Policies and Economic Development," in *Rural Economic Development in the 1980s: Preparing for the Future*, Agricultural and Rural Economy Division, Economic Research Service, U.S. Department of Agriculture, ERS Staff Report No. AGES-870724.

26. Autry, 1988, "Federal Neglect Crippling the Rural South."

27. Ibid.

28. Rosenfeld, Stuart A., 1983, "Prospects for Economic Growth in the Nonmetropolitan South," SGPB Alert (Research Triangle Park, NC).

29. Southern Growth Policies Board, 1985, "Looking Forward: Visions of the Future of the South" (Research Triangle Park, NC).

30. Wilson, William J., 1987, *The Truly Disadvantaged* (Chicago: University of Chicago Press), p. 151.

31. Ibid., pp. 151-52.

32. Southern Growth Policies Board, 1985, "Looking Forward," p. 20.

33. For a discussion of this issue, see William F. Fox, 1986, "Public Infrastructure and Economic Development," in *Rural Economic Development in the 1980's*.

34. Choate, Pat, and Susan Walter, 1984, "America in Ruins: The Decaying Infrastructure," in Michael Barker (ed.), *Rebuilding America's Infrastructure* (Durham, NC: Duke University Press).

35. Stocker, Frederick D., 1985, "Research Needs for Rural Public Services," Agricultural and Rural Economy Division, Economic Research Service, U.S. Department of Agriculture, ERS Staff Report No. AGES840822.

36. Fox, William F., 1986, "Public Infrastructure and Economic Development," p. 13-11.

37. For a discussion of the implications of New Federalism on infrastructure development, see Roger J. Vaughan, 1984, "Rebuilding America: Financing Public Works in the 1980s," in Barker (ed.), *Rebuilding America's Infrastructure*, pp. 100-330.

38. Choate and Walter, 1984, "America in Ruins," p. 71.

39. Ibid.

40. Bowles, Samuel, David M. Gordon, and Thomas E. Weiskopf, 1983, *Beyond the Wasteland* (New York: Anchor/Doubleday).

41. Obey, David R., 1986, "A Public Economics of Growth, Equity and Opportunity," in Obey and Sarbanes, *The Changing American Economy*, pp. 8-15.

42. Ibid.

43. Wilson, 1987, *The Truly Disadvantaged*, p. 121.

44. Lyson, Thomas A., 1981, "Meeting the Social and Economic Needs of Rural Americans: An Unfinished Agenda," *Journal of Intergroup Relations* 9(1): 17-23.

45. Ibid.

46. Ibid.

Bibliography

Auchmutey, Jim, and Priscilla Painton. 1986a. "Revenue Cutbacks Leave Region with a Thinner Thread of Hope," *Atlanta Constitution*, November 20.

——— . 1986b. "Rural Refugees Tote Their Troubles into Southern Cities," *Atlanta Constitution*, November 20.

Autry, George B. 1988. "Federal Neglect Crippling the Rural South," *Atlanta Journal/Constitution*, January 17.

Batra, Ravi, 1987. "An Ominous Trend to Greater Inequality," *New York Times*, May 3.

Beauchamp, Tom L. 1980. "Distributive Justice and the Difference Principle," in H. G. Blocker and E. H. Smith (eds.), *John Rawls' Theory of Social Justice*, Athens, OH: Ohio University Press, pp. 132-61.

Beaulieu, Lionel J. 1988. "The Rural South in Crisis: An Introduction," in L. J. Beaulieu (ed.), *The Rural South in Crisis*, Boulder, CO: Westview, pp. 1-12.

Beazley, J. Ernest, and Jacob M. Schlesinger. 1987. "Town Stunned by VW Plant's Closing Though End Had Been Long Expected," *Wall Street Journal*, November 23.

Bloomquist, Leonard E. 1987. "Performance of the Rural Manufacturing Sector," in *Rural Economic Development in the 1980s: Preparing for the Future*, Agriculture and Rural Economy Division, Economic Research Service, U.S. Department of Agriculture, ERS Staff Report No. AGES870724, pp. 3-1-3-33.

Bluestone, Barry, and Bennett Harrison. 1982. *The Deindustrialization of America*, New York: Basic Books.

——— . 1987. "The Grim Truth About the Job Miracle," *New York Times*, February 1.

Bluestone, Herman, and John Hession. 1986. "Patterns of Change in the Nonmetro and Metro Labor Force since 1979," in D. Jahr, J. Johnson, and R. Wimberely (eds.), *New Dimensions in Rural Policy: Building Upon Our Heritage*, Joint Economic Committee of the U.S. Congress, Washington, D.C.: U.S. Government Printing Office, pp. 121-33.

Bowles, Samuel, David M. Gordon, and Thomas E. Weiskopf. 1983. *Beyond the Wasteland*, New York: Anchor/Doubleday.

Briggs Jr., Vernon M., Brian S. Rungeling, and Lewis H. Smith. 1978. *Human Needs and Income Supplement Programs in the Rural South*, Center for Manpower Studies, University of Mississippi.

Chiccoine, David L., and Gordon A. Hoke. 1986. "Rural Economies, Tax Structures, and Meeting the Demand for State-Local Government Services: A Focus on Local Schools," in Jahr, Johnson, and Wimberely, (eds.), *New Dimensions in Rural Policy: Building Upon Our Heritage*, Joint Economic Committee of the U.S. Congress, Washington D.C.: U.S. Government Printing Office, pp. 450-60.

Choate, Pat, and Susan Walter. 1984. "America in Ruins: The Decaying Infrastructure," in Michael Barker (ed.), *Rebuilding America's Infrastructure*, Durham, NC: Duke University Press.

Cobb, James C. 1982. *The Selling of the South*, Baton Rouge: Louisiana State University Press.

———. 1984. *Industrialization and Southern Society 1877-1984*, Lexington, KY: University Press of Kentucky.

Cordes, S. M., and J. S. Wright. 1985. "Rural health concerns for the present and future," in J. Hamburg, D. J. Mase, and J. W. Perry (eds.), *Review of Allied Health Education*, Lexington, KY: University of Kentucky Press.

Deaton, Brady J., and Anne S. Deaton. 1988. "Educational Reform and Regional Development," in L. J. Beaulieu (ed.), *The Rural South in Crisis*, Boulder, CO: Westview, pp. 304-24.

England, Paula. 1981. "Assessing Trends in Occupational Sex Segregation, 1900-1976," in Ivar Berg (ed.), *Sociological Perspectives on Labor Markets*, New York: Academic Press, pp. 273-96.

Evanson, Elizabeth. 1984. "Employment Programs for the Poor: Government in the Labor Market," *Focus* 7(3).

Falk, W. W., and T. A. Lyson. 1988. *Hi-Tech, Low-Tech, No-Tech: Recent Occupational and Industrial Changes in the Rural and Urban South*, Albany: SUNY-Albany Press.

"50 Year Trend Reversed as U.S. Regions Grow Apart Economically," *New York Times*, August 23, 1987, p. 18.

Fox, William F. 1986. "Public Infrastructure and Economic Development," in *Rural Economic Development in the 1980s: Preparing for the Future*, Agricultural and Rural Economy Division, Economic Research Service, U.S. Department of Agriculture, ERS Staff Report No. AGES870724.

Gilder, George. 1981. *Wealth and Poverty*, New York: Basic Books.
Goldman, Holly Smith. 1980. "Rawls and Utilitarianism," in H. G. Blocker and E. H. Smith (eds.), *John Rawls Theory of Social Justice*, Athens, OH: Ohio University Press, pp. 346-94.
Goodman, Robert. 1979. *The Last Entrepreneurs*. New York: Simon and Schuster.
Hanna, Frank A. 1959. *State Income Differentials 1919-1954*, Durham, NC: Duke University Press.
Haren, Claude C., and Ronald W. Holling. 1979. "Industrial Development in Nonmetropolitan America: A Locational Perspective," in R. E. Lonsdale and H. L. Seyler (eds.), *Nonmetropolitan Industrialization*, New York: V. H. Winston and Sons, pp. 13-45.
Hirschl, Thomas A., Gene F. Summers, and Leonard E. Bloomquist. 1989. "Right to Work Legislation and Local Labor Market Growth," in W. W. Falk and T. A. Lyson (eds.) *Research in Rural Sociology and Development.* Volume 4: *Rural Labor Markets*, Greenwich, CT: JAI Press.
Horan, Patrick M., and Charles M. Tolbert. 1984. *The Organization of Work in Rural and Urban Labor Markets.* Boulder, CO: Westview Press.
Ingwerson, Marshall. 1986. "Japanese Firms Help South Rise Again," *Christian Science Monitor*, May 6.
James, Thomas E., Jr. 1983. "Anticipating Future Growth in the Sunbelt," in Steven C. Ballard and Thomas E. James (eds.), *The Future of the Sunbelt*, New York: Praeger Publishers, pp. 37-62.
Kale, Steven R. 1986. "Stability, Growth, and Adaptability to Economic and Social Change in Rural Labor Markets," in Molly S. Killian, Leonard E. Bloomquist, Shelley Pendelton, and David McGranahan (eds.), *Symposium on Rural Labor Markets Research Issues*, Economic Research Service, U.S. Department of Agriculture Staff Report AGES860721, Washington, D.C.: U.S. Government Printing Office, pp. 77-119.
Korsching, Peter F., and Stephen G. Sapp. 1978. "Unemployment Estimation in Rural Areas: A Critique of Official Procedures and a Comparison with Survey Data," *Rural Sociology* 43 (Spring), pp. 101-110.
Lee, John E. 1983. "Some Consequences of the New Reality in U.S. Agriculture," in D. E. Brewster, W. D. Rasmussen, and G. Youngberg (eds.), *Farms in Transition*, Ames, Iowa: Iowa State University Press, pp. 3-22.
Lichter, Daniel T. 1988. "Race and Underemployment: Black Employment Hardship in the South," in L. J. Beaulieu (ed.), *The Rural South in Crisis*, Boulder, CO: Westview, pp. 181-97.
Lichter, Daniel T., and Janice A. Costanzo. 1986. "Underemployment in Nonmetropolitan America, 1970-1982," in D. Jahr, J. Johnson, and R. Wimberely (eds.), *New Dimensions in Rural Policy: Building Upon Our*

Heritage, Joint Economic Committee of the U.S. Congress. Washington, D.C.: U.S. Government Printing Office, pp. 134-43.

Lyson, Thomas A. 1981. "Meeting the Social and Economic Needs of Rural Americans: An Unfinished Agenda," *Journal of Intergroup Relations*, 9(1), pp. 17-23.

———. 1985. "Race and Sex Segregation in the Occupational Structure of Southern Employers," *Social Science Quarterly*, 66(2), pp. 281-95.

———. 1986. "Entry into Farming: Implications of a Dual Agricultural Structure," in J. J. Molnar (ed.), *Agricultural Change: Consequences for Southern Farms and Rural Communities*. Boulder, CO: Westview, pp. 155-76.

Lyson, Thomas A., and Georganne McMullin. 1986. "The Changing Structure of South Carolina Agriculture Since 1959," Bulletin 655, Clemson, SC: South Carolina Agricultural Experiment Station, Clemson University.

Marshall, Ray. 1974. *Rural Workers in Rural Labor Markets*, Salt Lake City: Olympus Publishing Co.

Martin, James W. 1931. "Industrial Change and Taxation Problems in the Southern States," *Annals of the American Academy of Political and Social Science* 153 (January), pp. 224-37.

McKeating, Michael P. 1975. "New York Losing the Race for New Industry," *The Empire State Report* 1 (October), p. 378. Reprinted in Peter D. McClelland and Alan L. Magdovitz (1981), *Crisis in the Making*, Cambridge, MA: Cambridge University Press.

McKinlay, John B. (ed.). 1981. *Health Maintenance Organizations*, Cambridge, MA: MIT Press.

Moody's Investors Service, Inc. 1968. *Opportunity and Growth in South Carolina 1968-1985*. New York: Moody's Investor Service.

Myers, Greg. 1986. "States Wage Costly Wars for New Industries," *The Greenville News/Piedmont*, March 4.

National Conference of Catholic Bishops. 1986. Economic Justice for All, Publication No. 101, Washington, D.C.: U.S. Catholic Conference, Inc.

Naylor, Thomas H., and James Clotfelter. 1975. *Strategies for Change in the South*, Chapel Hill: University of North Carolina Press.

Obey, David R. 1986. "A Public Economics of Growth, Equity and Opportunity," in David R. Obey and Paul Sarbanes, *The Changing American Economy*, New York: Basil Blackwell.

Obey, David R., and Paul Sarbanes (eds.). 1986. *The Changing American Economy*, New York: Basil Blackwell.

Office of Technology Assessment. 1986. "Technology, Public Policy and the Changing Structure of Agriculture," Washington, D.C.: U.S. Government Printing Office.

Personick, Valerie. 1985. "A Second Look at Industry Output and Employment Trends Through 1995," *Monthly Labor Review*, 58 (November), pp. 12-19.

Pierce, Neil. 1979. "State 'Smokestack Chasing'—Barking Up the Wrong Tree?" *Washington Post*, June 3.
The President's National Advisory Commission on Rural Poverty. 1967. *The People Left Behind*, Washington, D.C.: U.S. Government Printing Office.
Rawls, John. 1971. *A Theory of Justice*, Cambridge, MA: Harvard University Press.
Reich, Robert. 1982. "Making Industrial Policy," *Foreign Affairs*, Spring.
———. 1983. *The Next American Frontier*, New York: Times Books.
Report. 1963. Arkansas Industrial Development Commission, Little Rock, Arkansas.
Rohatyn, Felix. 1981. "Reconstructing America," *New York Review of Books*, February 5.
Rosenfeld, Stuart A. 1983. "Prospects for Economic Growth in the Nonmetropolitan South," *SGPB Alert*, Research Triangle Park, NC.
———. 1988. "The Tale of Two Souths," in L. J. Beaulieu (ed.), *The Rural South in Crisis*, Boulder, CO: Westview.
Rosenfeld, Stuart A., Edward M. Bergmar, and Sarah Rubin. 1985. *After the Factories*. Research Triangle Park, NC: Southern Growth Policies Board.
Rosenthal, Robert, and Lenore Jacobson. 1968. *Pygmalion in the Classroom: Teacher Expectation and Pupil's Intellectual Development*, New York: Holt, Rinehart and Winston.
Ross, Peggy J., and Stuart A. Rosenfeld. 1987. "Human Resource Policies and Economic Development," in *Rural Economic Development in the 1980s: Preparing for the Future*, Agricultural and Rural Economy Division, Economic Research Service, U.S. Department of Agriculture, ERS Staff Report No. AGES870724.
Rungeling, Brian, Lewis H. Smith, Vernon M. Briggs, Jr., and John F. Adams. 1977. *Employment, Income and Welfare in the Rural South*. New York: Praeger.
"Saved from Mazda." 1985. *Greenville News*, January 11.
Schmidt, William E. 1986. "Not All of the South is in the Sunbelt." *New York Times*, January 19.
Shadows in the Sunbelt. 1986. A report of the MDC Panel on Rural Economic Development, Chapel Hill: MDC, Inc.
Southern Growth Policies Board. 1985. "Looking Forward: Visions of the Future of the South," Research Triangle Park, NC.
Southern Growth Policies Board, 1986. "Halfway Home and a Long Way to Go," Research Triangle Park, NC.
Stocker, Frederick D. 1985. "Research Needs for Rural Public Services," Agricultural and Rural Economy Division, Economic Research Service, U.S. Department of Agriculture, ERS Staff Report No. AGES840822.
Suitts, Steve, 1986. "Poverty in the South," in Lucy R. Watkins (ed.) *Equity: The Critical Link in Southern Economic Development*, Research Triangle Park, NC: Southern Growth Policies Board, pp. 21-24.

Thompson, Wilbur. 1965. *A Preface to Urban Economics*, Baltimore: The Johns Hopkins Press.

―――. 1969. "The Economic Base of Urban Problems," in Neil W. Chamberlain (ed.), *Contemporary Economic Issues*, Homewood, IL: Richard D. Irwin, pp. 1-47.

Thurow, Lester C. 1987. "A Surge in Inequality," *Scientific American*, 236(5), pp. 30-37.

Tolbert, Charles M. 1989. "Labor Market Areas in Stratification Research: Concepts, Definitions, and Issues," in W. W. Falk and T. A. Lyson (eds.) *Research in Rural Sociology and Development, Volume 4, Rural Labor Markets*, Greenwich, CT: JAI Press.

Tolbert, Charles M., and Molly Sizer Killean. 1987. "Labor Market Areas in the United States," Economic Research Service, United States Department of Agriculture, Washington, D.C.

U.S. Bishops' Pastoral Letter on Catholic Social Teaching and the U.S. Economy. 1984. First Draft published in *Origins* 14(22/23), November 15.

Vass, Kathy. 1986. "TEC Tailors Classes to Industries' Needs," *Greenville News/Piedmont*, May 11.

Vaughan, Roger J. 1984. "Rebuilding America: Financing Public Works in the 1980s," in Michael Barker (ed.), *Rebuilding America's Infrastructure*, Durham, NC: Duke University Press.

Walsh, Susan M., and Craig M. Wheeland. 1984. "Tax Incentives for Industrial and Economic Development," in C. B. Graham, Jr. and C. B. Tyer (eds.), *Local Government in South Carolina: Problems and Perspectives*, Columbia, SC: University of South Carolina, Bureau of Governmental Research and Service, pp. 153-70.

Wilkinson, Kenneth P. 1984. "Implementing a National Strategy of Rural Development," *Rural Sociologist*, 4(5), p. 351.

Wilson, William J. 1987. *The Truly Disadvantaged*. Chicago: University of Chicago Press.

Wright, J. Stephen, and Dale W. Lick. 1986. "Health in Rural America: Problems and Recommendations," in D. Jahr, J. Johnson, and R. Wimberely (eds.), *New Dimensions in Rural Policy: Building Upon Our Heritage*, Joint Economic Committee of the U.S. Congress, Washington, DC: U.S. Government Printing Office, pp. 461-69.

Index

agriculture, 42-43, 74, 78, 103, 110; agribusiness, 107, 112; farmers, 42-43, 103; farm workers, 106-107; part-time farmers, 103, 107
Arkansas Industrial Development Commission, 13
Autry, George B., 125-26

Batra, Ravi, 118
Beauchamp, Tom L., 14
Beaulieu, Lionel J., 2-3
blacks, 3, 25-26, 52, 60
Bloomquist, Leonard E., 90
Bluestone, Barry, 118
Bowles, Samuel, 131

Choate, Pat, 129-30
Clotfelter, James, 32
Cobb, James C., 10

Deaton, Brady J., 124
de facto industrial policy, 4-11, 15-16

Economic development, 1-2, 120-35

education, 50; attainment, 3, 50; segregation, 52-53, 58; teachers, 58; vocational training, 126
employment opportunities, 43
Evanson, Elizabeth, 124

Falk, William W., 16
female-headed households, 67-69
Fox, William F., 129
full employment, 131-32

Gilder, George, 124
Goldman, Holly Smith, 15
Goodman, Robert, 6-7
Gordon, David M., 131
government, 46, 120-23; federal, and education, 55; and equity and justice programs, 130-35; and human resource development, 123-27; and infrastructure development, 129-30; and welfare reform, 133-34; local, 55, 123; state, 55, 123

Harrison, Bennett, 118
Hawkins, Augustus, 133

healthcare, 58-67; dentists, 64; physicians, 64
Health Maintenance Organizations, 63-64
high technology employment, 90-91, 102-103
Horan, Patrick M., 16
human resource development, 49, 123-27; CETA, 124-25; JPTA, 124-25

Income, 1, 3, 32
industrial composition, 75-78
industrial recruiters, 13
industrial recruiting/incentives: industrial revenue bonds, 4-5; tax abatements, 4-5; other, 4-5
infant mortality, 2
infrastructure, 127-30

justice, economic, 11-16, 47; social, 11-16, 70; policy and programs, 130-34

Kennedy, Edward, 133

Labor market areas, 16-22; education trends, 52-58; healthcare, 60-67; high technology employment, 91; income rates, 33-36; industrial composition, 75-78; manufacturing employment, 79-84; manufacturing wages, 37-39; occupational segregation in the high-technology sector, 102-103; occupational segregation in the manufacturing sector, 96-97; occupational segregation in the service sector, 97-101; poverty rates, 29-31; race and sex segregation, 93-96; service sector employment, 84-90; service sector wages, 39-41; underemployment rates, 44-45; unemployment rates, 41-43; welfare, 67-69
Lyson, Thomas A., 16

Manufacturing, 96-97; employment, 73, 79-84; wages, 36-39, 79-84
Marshall, Ray, 123

National capital budget, 130
National Conference of Catholic Bishops, 14-15, 122
national industrial policy, 117
Naylor, Thomas H., 32
New Federalism, 127, 129

Obey, David R., 122, 131
occupational composition, 75-78
occupational segregation, 96-103; race, 93-96; sex, 93-96
Office of Technology Assessment, 120, 123
Osborne, David, 117

Phillips, Pete, 46
poverty, 1-3, 25-31, 67-69
product cycle, 36-37
property taxes, 54-57

Quality of life, 2

Rawls, John, 13-14
Rosenfeld, Stuart A., 118, 126

Sarbanes, Paul, 122
service industries, 75, 97-101; employment, 84-90; wages, 84-90
Shadows in the Sunbelt, 116
Southern Growth Policies Board, 31, 126-27
states: Alabama, 4; Arkansas, 13; Georgia, 46; Kentucky, 4-5; Louisiana, 33; Mississippi, 4, 26,

33, 50; New York, 12; North Carolina, 30; Pennsylvania, 117; South Carolina, 5-6, 12
Suits, Steve, 31

Thompson, Wilbur, 75
Thurow, Lester C., 118
Tolbert, Charles M., 16-17

Underemployment, 41, 43
unemployment, 41-43, 125
unions/unionization, 7, 10

utilitarianism, 15-16

Wages, 31, 132-33; manufacturing, 6, 36-39; service sector, 39
Walter, Susan, 129-30
Weiskopf, Thomas E., 131
welfare, 67-69; payments, 133-34; programs, 133-34
whites, 26, 28, 54, 60
Wilkinson, Kenneth P., 122
Wilson, William J., 126, 131-32

ABOUT THE AUTHOR

THOMAS A. LYSON holds a teaching and research position in the Department of Rural Sociology at Cornell University. He received his Ph.D. in 1976 from Michigan State University and worked briefly as a labor analyst for the State of Michigan. Between 1977 and 1986 he was a faculty member in the Department of Agricultural Economics and Rural Sociology at Clemson University. He is co-author, with William W. Falk, of *High Tech, Low Tech, No Tech: Recent Industrial and Occupational Change in the South*. He is currently working on a study of recent organizational and technological changes in the American dairy industry.